Healing the
Heartbreak of
Grief

Healing the Heartbreak of Grief

Peter James Flamming

Abingdon Press
Nashville

HEALING THE HEARTBREAK OF GRIEF

Library of Congress Cataloging-in-Publication Data

Flamming, Peter James, 1934-
    Healing the heartbreak of grief / Peter James Flamming.
        p. cm.
    Includes bibliographical references.
    ISBN 978-1-4267-0221-1 (pbk. : alk. paper)
    1. Grief—Religious aspects—Christianity. 2. Bereavement—Religious aspects—Christianity. 3. Loss (Psychology)—Religious aspects—Christianity. I. Title.
    BV4905.3.F53 2010
    248.8'66—dc22

                                                                        2009024268

10 11 12 13 14 15 16 17 18 19—10 9 8 7 6 5 4 3 2 1

MANUFACTURED IN THE UNITED STATES OF AMERICA

To the Memory and Joy of
Peter Dave Flamming

Contents

Introduction

Grief happens. It is part of life. Because it often comes in small doses, we don't readily identify it as grief. But it is there. You are in the third grade when your closest friend tells you she is moving because her father has been transferred. Your first response is, "No! Tell me it's not true." But it is true and you feel the loss keenly. Still, you replace that friend, and she finds new friends in her new location.

But in this book grief walks the road called heartbreak. We are dealing with irrevocable loss. What has been can never be again. We may have lost someone we have deeply loved. Or we may be facing health adjustments we never could have imagined happening to us. I think of wounded veterans whose lives are changed forever. No word, no phrase can carry the true burden of what is felt. We feel as if we are dying inside. It is like someone has hit us with a blow that has taken all of the life, the hope, and the future away from us.

With this kind of heartbreaking grief you likely have had no experience. It is like being lost in a forest you've never visited, on roads you've never traveled, toward a destination you know not where. The inner pain of loss is so intense that you are at first numb. You may think, *This is the sort of thing that happens to others but not to me, not to us*. But there you are. It has happened. You are apt to ask yourself, *How am I going to make it through this?* That is what this book is about.

My sharing with you about grief comes from three sources. First, I took a keen interest in grief during my graduate studies. Fortunately, a large amount of study and research has gone into understanding grief. Second, I have been a pastor for more than fifty years, walking with others through their grief experiences. Third, my wife, Shirley, and I lost our thirty-three-year-old son to leukemia. Married with three children, Dave was in graduate school at the University of Texas when he began to have a pain in his leg. He went to the Health Center at the university. When they did some blood work, they discovered he had leukemia. He and his wonderful young family came to Richmond, Virginia, where I was pastor. He received treatment at the Massey Cancer Center. For fifteen months we fought it. His brother Douglas provided a bone marrow transplant. We all thought we had won the battle. But it was not to be. When it turned, it turned in a fury, and we lost him. We began walking a road we had never walked before, feeling emotions and despair we had never felt before. We began to live out the question, *How are we going to make it through this?*

As time passed, I began to experience the healing side of grief. I learned by trial and error that there were some important steps to take in turning the grief experience into a healing experience. These steps do not necessarily come in a predictable order. But they are crucial, and that is what this book is about.

I will also introduce you to a phrase that you may not have heard before: the wisdom of grief. I believe that wisdom is at work in the process of healing. It is usually unnoticed. But the wisdom of grief is quietly transforming things whether we are aware of it or not. We will be looking at that in the first chapter. I trust that this book may be a healing experience for you.

This book was not intended to be read straight through, as you would read most books. As you deal with your heartbreaking grief, take your time. Read this book in bits and pieces, one chapter at a time. When you have finished, return to those chapters which are the most helpful.

One further word. Grief often begins as a family experience. But every person in the family handles grief in a singular way. Every family member needs to be allowed to work through deep grief in his or her own way.

I would like to express my appreciation to my family members, who have walked with me through this experience. My gratitude embraces the churches I have been privileged to serve and, especially, the people with whom I have walked through sorrow. Dr. Joe Bauserman was my counselor. He was like a pastor to me during my darkest times. For his guidance I am eternally grateful. My deep appreciation goes to Dr. Kathryn Armistead, without whose guidance this book never would have come about.

Dr. Peter James Flamming
Richmond, Virginia

CHAPTER ONE

When Grief
Breaks In

G *rief* is a heavy word. I know of no way to lighten its load upon our hearts. But before we begin to speak of the challenges of grief and how we will get through them, let me begin with helpful and positive words concerning what grief is about.

WHAT GRIEF IS ABOUT

Grief is to the inner self what the healing systems of the body are to the physical self. Just as the body has many systems that allow the physical self to heal when the body has been through trauma, so grief is one of the vital systems of the inner self that allows the emotional and relational parts of us to heal.

Suppose you were in a train wreck. You survived but received significant physical injuries. The physicians and surgeons did what

1

needed to be done to help you not only survive but also heal and recover. Pain was part of the journey. Patience was needed. There were high times and low times. Sometimes you cried, sometimes you smiled, but always you hurt. But eventually, at a pace slower than you anticipated, you walked and smiled and worked again. The physicians and surgeons were indispensable agents of healing. The truth is that their task was to create the right conditions in which your body could heal itself. God created the body with healing systems that immediately go to work when trauma happens, especially if they are given help from those who know how to help.

When you have lost someone you dearly love, you feel as if you have been in an emotional and relational train wreck. Your whole world crashes around you. The sharp, stabbing pain you feel on the inside may be invisible to others, but it is constantly present within you. Your heart is broken, and no heart doctor can heal it.

This is where grief comes in. Grief is the heart doctor. Of course, it is not a physical heart doctor but an emotional, relational, and even spiritual heart doctor. Grief is an invisible healer. As painful and even horrible as it sometimes feels, grief eventually heals us enough so that we can begin again. It is the inner heart system that eventually helps us put life back together again. But this heart system embraces deep and painful emotions related to our loss. The positive wisdom of grief seeks to take the awful pain of our loss and eventually redeem or recycle it for our good. We will probably not sense this when we are going through such painful grief. But looking back, we realize that a quiet transformation has taken place. For instance, we will see how grief will tenderly transform the terrible loss that we experience into a tribute to the one for whom we grieve.

The key point here is for you to adjust your vision so that you can see the invisible but positive power of grief—grief as a healer. Grief is your friend, not your enemy. The inner pain will be intense. You will need immense amounts of patience. There will be many low times, sometimes even depressive times. Recovery will come much slower than you wish. The sharp, stabbing—but inner—pain that is the signature of grief will seldom leave you alone. But through it all, keep believing that silently and invisibly, grief is doing its work of recovery, because it is.

THAT IRREVERSIBLE TRAGIC MOMENT

One thing we have in common. For all of us, our journey with heartbreaking grief began with what might be called an irreversible tragic moment. At that moment, what has been is gone forever. It is a tragedy of indescribable loss. One loved and treasured is gone. Even if we are skilled with words, we likely can find no word or phrase to describe the feeling of being torn apart by the loss.

How did it happen with you? It might have been when you received the phone call that the tragedy had happened. Or it might have been the word from the physician that your loved one was in a coma and the end was near. Or maybe there was a knock at the door with the news that nobody wanted to deliver to you.

But someone did. Your world changed forever. It is that moment when the one you have loved is gone and the future you had longed for is no longer possible.

That tragic, irreversible moment, that moment that seems to change everything, we are apt to remember for the rest of our lives, even down to the last detail. We do not talk about it, because it is too painful, even after many years. Besides, people would think we never moved beyond our loss. Yet we remember. We remember where we were. If others were present, they too become part of the memory. We might even remember what they were wearing and where they were sitting or standing. We are apt to recall what words were said and how we responded.

In my younger years, an older Jewish tailor became a good friend of mine. One day after he had fitted me for a new suit, I noticed the tattooed numbers on his arm. I asked him about them. After pausing a moment, almost as if he was gathering himself, he shared with me that, as a young adult, he had been incarcerated in one of Hitler's death camps in Germany. The tattoo was his number. Following an extended silence, I asked him if his experience still bothered him. Had he been able to forget? His reply was simple but painful. He said, "Many nights I wake up and remember some part of it. When that happens, I am so glad when day comes and I can go to work and forget it all for a little while." Those memories were at least forty years old by that time.

The rest of the grief experience, the period of healing and recovery, will weave itself into our lives. When we look back at the healing epoch of our grief, our memories will more or less run together. But the tragic, irreversible moment becomes a permanent memory. It becomes part of who we are and who we become.

So if you are troubled or puzzled about why you remember so vividly what happened on that day, the reason is that we remember the tragic moments of our lives. There is nothing wrong with you or your emotional health if you remember those moments, hours, and days.

THE WORLD GOES RIGHT ON

One of the abrupt and painful realities you will face is that the world goes right on as if nothing has happened.

Your whole life has been torn apart. An invisible emotional and relational hemorrhage is bleeding inside you. Except for the immediate sympathy of those closest to us, nobody seems to notice or care. A mother said to me after her son died of cancer, "I go to the grocery store, and everything goes on just as if nothing has happened. I want to stand at the door and scream, 'Don't you know what has happened? My son is gone. His future is gone. His promise is gone. His wife has no husband and his children have no father. Our lives have changed forever, and you go on gathering your groceries as if none of this matters.'"

I remember when our son Dave died after such a gallant fight against leukemia. A nice article appeared in the newspaper in addition to the obituary. I went to the barbershop to get a haircut before the memorial service. My barber had read the article and said, "I'm sorry about your son." Another barber nodded. There was a brief moment of pause, which I deeply appreciated. Then everything went right on as usual. Clip, clip, clip. In truth, that is what should have happened. One cannot expect a funeral wreath to be hung on the door of the barbershop because one of its customers has suffered a death in the family. But I cannot tell you how much it hurt. My son had died. His wife was now a widow. His girls were without a father. Our lives were changed forever. But the barbershop went on just as if nothing important had happened, clip, clip, clip.

While you are trying to let grief do its work, one challenge facing you is that the culture, the society in which you live, is not prone to help you. Oh, people will respond sympathetically during the immediate crisis. But the culture of which you are a part has a short interest span. People will expect you to be free of your grief as soon as possible and get on with your life. The world in which you live has little patience with grief.

In former days and in other cultures, a woman whose husband had died would wear black for months, maybe a year. Doing this may seem depressing to us. But the wonderful thing was that it made valid the grief she was feeling; she was not expected to be over and done with it in a brief time. In the popular view of our society, grief should certainly take no longer than a year at the most. In truth, after one year, you will have learned how to function, how to say the right words at the right time, how to smile instead of weep. But deep inside, you may well be grieving just as intensely as ever. Grief will be doing its healing, transforming work when most people will have forgotten that anything happened.

"Get over it and forget about it" is more their message than "stick with it."

The purpose of this book is to help you stick with it. The world of which you are a part will not be there to cheer you on.

GRIEF IS AT WORK

A hidden purpose of grief is to take the sharp edges of loss and soften them. Grief is not only a healer. It also transforms things. It does so in a gradual but soft and wise way if we will let it.

For example, grief can transform things by what it does to the finality of everything. Nicholas Wolterstorff calls this the *neverness* of what has happened.

Nicholas's son, Eric, was twenty-five years old when he fell to his death while mountain climbing. In the dreadful aftermath of the loss of Eric, Nicholas kept a journal of his thoughts and his sorrow. Eventually he published these reflections under the title *Lament for a Son*. In one of those he wrote:

> It's the *neverness* that is so painful. *Never again* to be here with us—never to sit with us at table, never to travel with us, never to laugh with us, never to cry with us, never to embrace us as he leaves for school, never to see his brothers and sister marry. All the rest of our lives we must live without him.[1]

I think of the loss of our son. For fifteen months we had fought the leukemia with the faith and hope of total recovery. Then, in a rapid reversal, he came out of remission. It all happened so fast, and then he was gone. Suddenly Betsy, his wife, was a widow; their three daughters were without their father; my wife, Shirley, and I were suddenly the parents of two sons, not three. His two brothers felt brotherless. The great potential of his life came to an end. He had significant musical talent, but the songs he wrote, the melodies he sang, were silent. I could go on and on. But when you have suffered such great loss, everything is so sudden and so completely final. As Wolterstorff puts it, "It's the *neverness* that is so painful."

A Transforming Tribute

What does the tender wisdom of grief do to the neverness of what has happened? Don't misunderstand. The wisdom of grief will never make light of your inner devastation. Grief will not blunt the reality of what has happened. But it will seek to transform it.

The wisdom of grief softly and quietly asks questions: "Would you really like to be able to just walk on as if nothing had happened? Would you like to live as if that person's place in your life really didn't matter? What would it really say about your love for that person if you could just yawn and move on?" The wisdom of grief whispers, "Don't you see that part of the intense pain of your grief is your tribute to the one you have loved and lost? It is your salute to a life well lived, a commendation and blessing for the one you remember with such devotion."

The wisdom of grief has a way of allowing the one who is gone to never be forgotten. One way we can embrace these memories is to create rituals of tribute. One of ours is to light a candle every Sunday on a little altar in our house. Someone might say, "That is a needless reminder of your loss." We would reply, "It is our sustained tribute to one we loved so deeply." Rituals of tribute are important.

Anniversaries play a key role here, even though they are painful. As you anticipate a key grief anniversary date, you will feel the heaviness days before. But when the anniversary arrives, it will quietly salute the significance of the life that was lived and the love that both of you cherished.

Christmas will be difficult every year. But in its own way, the heart-hurt that happens is an eternal tribute to the one you have lost. A way to mediate the loss that you feel is to make a gift in memory of and tribute to the one you have lost.

The wisdom of grief is also telling you something about yourself and your relationship with the one you lost. Listen to it and treasure it. Just as your grief pain is a tribute to the one you have lost, it is also a tribute to you. In a way, the loss that you feel is a precious jewel. It is a tribute to the relationship that you have shared and the love that you have given. It hurts so much, yet it also honors the bond that was yours.

From Closure to Possibility

The wisdom of grief, in its own slow way, is doing *one more essential thing* in its work of transformation of the neverness of your loss. It will use the finality of your loss to eventually redirect your attention from what has been to what can be. The finality of what has happened, ever so slowly, provides some closure to what has been and begins to point to the horizons of what can be. Without a measure of closure you cannot move from the past to the future.

But the closure comes with such tenderness that it never erases the tributes or the memories from what has been. It builds a bridge from the self that was to the self that can be. It will take time, sometimes a long time. But you are called to get on with your life without forgetting the one who is gone.

A Warning

Now, you can stop the wise and healing power of grief if you choose to. Granger Westberg tells about the rich widow whose musician husband died twenty years ago. She has kept his music studio just as he left it when he died. She has locked the keyboard of his piano. For twenty years the piano has played no tune or issued forth with any music. Each day she stands for a long time in the doorway with her memories. She has consistently refused to reenter life. She has become known as "that eccentric old lady."

Westberg remarks that she never wrestled her way to a new way of life. Apparently, she had few or no friends who were willing to stay by her side and help her walk through the "valley of the shadow." She felt that her only friend was her deceased husband, and she was dedicated to remain loyal to him. She wanted no one ever to play that piano again, lest she would be disloyal to the memory of her husband.[2]

The truth is that the tragedy in losing her husband was made more serious by her own tragedy. She was in some way meant to eventually make music with her life. *She refused by building a fortress around her memories.* It may be that no one will ever play that piano with the expertise that he did. But the piano was meant to be played. The music was meant to be heard. Part of the music was to be hers. Part of the music is to become ours as well.

The way to keep from building a fortress around our memories is to turn our memories into tributes and eventually to make music with our lives.

HELPING THE HEALING

In this chapter I have said that the great invisible helper and healer is grief. It is a gift, though many would refuse it if they could because of the pain that goes with it. But grief, though we might not choose it, is a gift from God. As the physical body has God-given systems to help it through trauma, so also does emotional and relational trauma have the healing system of grief. It works silently and is accompanied by great inner pain, but it has wisdom and healing power all its own. We can learn to be patient with it, trust it, and believe in it.

In your pain seek help beyond yourself. In the Christian faith the cross is the primary symbol. We Christians have decorated it, polished it, made jewelry out of it. Yet its basic truth remains: it is a symbol of great pain and suffering. Perhaps anticipating our heartbreaking times, Jesus instructed us to take up our own cross daily and follow him (Luke 9:23). For a Christian, heartbreaking grief becomes the healing cross that one carries day by day. The healing comes with the awareness that the Lord is walking with us, day by day, step by step. He has been there. He knows what grief is all about. He uses the process of grief to put us together again.

But don't forget the source of healing inside you. It is the grief process itself. As with physical healing, the healing of the grief process is invisible and does not depend upon your concentration. Even if you cannot think things through, fix them, or busy them out, you can trust that the God-given emotion of grief is doing its work on your behalf.

Remember, please, that *healing is a process, not an event*. It takes time. If you will believe it is happening and be patient with its work, healing will happen. The challenge now is how to encourage the healing process of grief within you. A basic and early question is *What do I do now?* To that we now turn.

****

This I Can Do Today:

I can light a candle in tribute to the one I have lost.

This I Can Remember Today:

I can remember that grief is an invisible healer.

CHAPTER TWO

What Do I Do Now?

Grief has entered. In the past days and weeks you have functioned as well as you can. You have made arrangements and said the right things. You have welcomed guests and friends who have come to stand by your side during your grief time. But they are returning to their private worlds, returning to their schedules and routines. They should. They have lives to live and duties to fulfill. Family members may still be around, but even so, you begin to feel alone. *Grief is not a group activity.*

So, what about you? The normal rhythms of life have been shattered. The patterns of life upon which you have always depended have been totally interrupted. In your quiet moments you are beginning to come to grips with a devastating truth: what has been is gone. However much you have grasped that with your mind, you are now beginning to feel its pain in your heart. You have suffered heartbreaking loss. The finality of it all breaks in at unexpected times and leaves you desolate.

In addition, exhaustion is your partner. Although each one of us handles grief in unique and different ways, we seem to have this in common. We live short on energy. We are numb. We move slowly. Some of the time we don't want to move at all. We don't want to be that way. But sometimes we seem unable to do anything about it.

A question that is likely to enter your mind is *What do I do now?*

Earlier we noticed the overlooked truth that grief carries within its folds some amazing wisdom. Some of that wisdom comes to us when we ask *What do I do now?* The answer is to adopt three healing practices that can actively keep you going. It is possible that you have had no practice with any of the three. It is also likely that you may need to return to the three time and time again, for grief can be a long journey. We will discuss them in turn.

FIRST: DO THE NEXT THING

For many, one of the first defeating realities of loss is inner exhaustion. Responsibilities are yours, and you must take care of them. Yet inertia sets in, and you don't feel like doing anything. Now the wisdom of grief has a healing answer. It whispers in the ears of your heart, "Just do the next thing." It doesn't have to be a big thing; whatever it is, just do it. When you do the next thing, two good things happen. The first is that something gets done, likely something that is essential. The second is that you turn your attention from your grief to the task at hand. In so doing you give your emotions a breather. *Tasking gives your emotions a rest.* They need some time out.

Essential responsibilities require your attention at times in your grief walk. You may still need to sign things or arrange for things or take care of matters relating to what you have experienced. You can put them off just so long. So, what do you do? Do you go to bed and pull the covers over your head and hide from everybody and everything? That won't work for long. They will come looking for you. Besides, you are not a quitter. So what do you do? *You do the next thing.* There is great healing in doing whatever seems to be the next thing to do.

A story from the Bible helped me here. After Jesus died, the Apostle Simon Peter must have felt devastated. Maybe even more so. His personal holocaust of grief was made the more devastating because of his huge guilt. Along with Judas, he was the great betrayer. He was accused of being part of the Jesus crowd, and he tried to lie his way out of it. The night of betrayal it came to be known. When Christians celebrate Communion, sometimes called the Lord's Supper or the Eucharist (Eucharist means "thanksgiving"), the scripture reading often begins, "On the night he was betrayed, Jesus took the bread and broke it . . ." "On the night he was betrayed." Judas and Simon Peter were the betrayers. Simon changed; Judas took his own life. How did Simon Peter make it?

Simon Peter went home to Galilee. Then he *did the next thing.* He said simply, "I am going out to fish" (John 21:3 NCV). It was the obvious next thing since that was his vocation; the sea was his workplace. To have done so, he needed to mend the nets, clean the boat, adjust the sails. Fishing for most of us is a sport or recreation. But Simon fished for a living. It was second nature for him to put his nets in the water. Fishing was the next thing he thought of doing. Incredibly, the risen Christ met him and his companions when he did. In fact, Jesus prepared breakfast for them. One of the great conversations of Scripture took place because of this, as recorded in John 21.

The Healing Power of Tasks

Here we have bumped into grief's wisdom teaching us about the healing power of tasks. When we do these tasks, we don't have to be industrious or goal setters. We don't have to be creative. *All we have to do is to set a time and a place and just show up.* In turning our attention to the tasks at hand, we turn our inner selves away from the memories and the pain of our loss for a time. An island of relief happens.

What is doing the next thing for you? Often it is whatever first comes to mind. It could be washing dishes, getting dressed, putting on your makeup, shaving, making the bed, doing the laundry, vacuuming the carpet, writing a letter, or cooking a meal. If you are able-bodied, it might mean going back to work or going for a walk. It might be paying the bills or calling a friend. Whatever comes to mind, do it. You probably won't feel like it, but do it. Don't prioritize. Just do whatever comes to mind. There is healing in that.

Let me repeat this because it is so important. In the heaviest of times, the wisdom of grief sends us out to do a task that needs doing. We won't usually feel like it. But two good things result.

Something that needs doing gets done. In addition, in tasking we rest our grief emotions for a while.

Likely you are sitting down while you are reading this. If the inertia of grief is about to drown you, put this book down and do the next thing. Grief is a marathon, not a sprint. But even a marathon begins with a single step. What is the first step? *Just do the thing that is at hand.*

SECOND: DON'T EXPECT TOO MUCH OF YOURSELF

Visiting hours were over, and the waiting room was almost empty. It was the day after we had gotten the mind-shattering news that Dave, our son who was in graduate school at the University of Texas, had leukemia. We had dropped everything to go to Austin to be with him; his wife, Betsy; and their three daughters. Now, for the first of countless times, we sat in a hospital reception area—waiting.

It was Sunday, and the only other person in the room was a kind, middle-aged woman. As I paced, she said to us, "You are distressed and I am sorry."

I nodded. "Our son has just been diagnosed as having leukemia. He is getting his first chemo here in Austin before we move him to Richmond, where we live."

"He is fortunate to have a family," she said. "I live alone and I am the one who has cancer. I wish I could tell you something that would help, but words don't help much and often hurt."

I nodded again. No answer was necessary.

I could not sit, so I paced while we waited. My pacing soon brought me back alongside the woman in the waiting room. Any other time I would have asked for her name and written it down. That day, I am embarrassed to admit, I didn't even ask.

The woman again interrupted the silence of the waiting room: "Since your son is just beginning his treatment, let me tell you the one thing that has helped me the most. Lower your expectations of yourself. Scale everything back. Nothing is at it used to be. Don't expect it to be."

She paused as if to remember a time in her past. "I remember when I kept my home spotless. I never left a dish in the sink. The furniture was always dusted." Again she stopped to remember, and as if she was speaking to herself, she added, "That seems like another lifetime."

I was about to ask what she did now when she said, "Now I just do what I can. The rest has to wait. The chemo just wipes me out for days. But I have learned one thing. I'm the only one who seems to notice how much doesn't get done. I didn't know until now that being squeaky clean was my priority. Nobody else seems to notice or care."

She took a deep breath as if she were ready to sum things up, which she was. "So just let things go. Don't expect as much of yourself. It is not a time to be a perfectionist."

I have thought about that advice many times since then: "So just let things go. Don't expect as much of yourself. It is not a time to be a perfectionist."

For many of us this is a strange way to approach life. We have prized getting things done, moving ahead, and setting new goals. Someday we will be there again. But we are not there now, and we need to make an attitude adjustment. Think through what *absolutely must* be done in comparison to what you would ordinarily think *should* be done. Many *shoulds* are of our own making. Let them go. Your day has enough heaviness without the added weight of unnecessary expectations.

THIRD: ADOPT AN ATTITUDE OF SURVIVAL

The third adjustment that the wisdom of grief asks us to make is this: adopt an attitude of survival. This sounds strange, even out of place. You live in a world where gaining high achievements is the goal, being ahead of others is the motivation, winning is supreme. There is nothing wrong with any of these at the right time and the right place. But you've been in an emotional train wreck. This is the time for healing. We visit many places along the journey of grief. But one of the most important for me was to adopt a seemingly simple attitude—*to survive, and to survive long enough to once again be hopeful.*

A man in the Old Testament was named Job. His story is told in an Old Testament book that bears his name. It is located almost in the middle of the Bible. Everything bad happened to Job. Had he been a cynic and a criminal, that might have made sense. But Job was the best of the best. Yet he lost everything and everyone. Some years ago Rabbi Harold Kushner wrote a book titled *When Bad Things Happen to Good People*.[1] Job was one of his prime examples.

Job went through a terribly difficult time of grief, and three friends came to help him. As long as they kept their mouths shut, their presence helped. Then they began to spin judgmental theology about why all of those dreadful things were happening to Job. In so doing they added to the trauma. But eventually Job survived—and with hope. In a huge expression of faith he exclaimed that he knew his Redeemer was still active in his world and in his life. He affirmed that the day would come when he would once again know God, experience God's presence, and things would work out (Job 19:25-27). They did work out. His hope was rewarded.

The book bearing his name is probably the most remarkable grief book in the Bible. Job survived with hope, and so can you. But your first commitment is to make it through—to survive.

At the End of Her Rope

Turn with me now from Job to a friend I will call Ann. The words came slowly, haltingly, with long pauses between the phrases. It was as if she was trying to express a pain so deep that no words could carry the freight of her desperation. Her words of pain were being transported on the tears that reflected what she had been through.

Ann had come to see me partly because she knew I had lost a son to leukemia and partly because she was desperate. "I can't take any more," she said. "I just can't handle another day. I'm at the end of my rope. I've never been here before. I have always been the strong one. What am I going to do? I want to go to sleep and never wake up."

When her tears subsided for a time, I said, "Don't worry about the future. Don't worry about what people think. The only thing important just now is for you to survive. You will feel you can no longer cope. You will feel you just are not able to go on. The pain will be so great, you will think you can no longer bear it. But for your sake and those you love, you must say to yourself, *I am going to survive. Nothing makes sense to me right now. But one thing I must do even if I don't feel like it. I need to make it through.*"

What do we do when the inner pain of loss is so intense it completely dominates everything? What do we do when the unthinkable has happened?

There is one basic gift that you need to give yourself and your loved ones. *You need to make the gritty, courageous inner decision to survive.* While you are making the decision to survive, add one more essential item: *keep at it until you can survive with hope.*

Arranging for Survival

The first step in surviving is to make some changes that allow you to handle where you are. Whatever arrangements need to be made, make them. Whatever scheduling needs to be changed, change it. Whatever help needs to be gotten, get it. If funds have been set aside for a rainy day, *this is the rainy day!* If you are completely exhausted, call someone to help you for a few days. If you have always handled everything yourself and suddenly you can't anymore, don't be too proud to call your pastor or a friend or family members or a counselor.

Read this carefully: *it is absolutely crucial that you survive. Everything and everyone gets worse if you don't.* Do things eventually get better? The answer is yes, but only if you survive. Eventually the pain will become less intense, and you will want to live again. But Ann Kaiser Stearns put it perfectly when she wrote, "Recovery begins with doing whatever is necessary for survival."[2] I would add, survival with hope.

****

This I Can Do Today:

I can do the next thing that needs to be done.

This I Can Remember Today:

In trying to survive, I can remember not to expect too much of myself. This is no time to be a perfectionist.

CHAPTER THREE

Unpredictable Emotions of Grief

Grief is such an emotional journey. Even familiar emotions intensify to such an extent, we are overwhelmed. In addition, we must begin to handle feelings we may never have felt before, such as the deep sadness that comes with irreplaceable loss. Some days we do not have emotions; our emotions have us.

EVELYN

A mother I shall call Evelyn had experienced the tragic loss of a child. It had turned into an emotional tsunami for her. She virtually withdrew from all of her friends, who were deeply concerned about her. One of them called and asked if I would see her even though she was not a member of any church. I agreed although I did not think she would come. She had never talked with any minister, much less during the loss she had experienced. But she did come, perhaps out of desperation.

Embarrassed at having to come to see me, she was hesitant and awkward at first. As she began to feel more confident, she shared that she had always been able to handle the challenges of life. Why not now? For the first time in her life there were moments she really didn't want to keep on living. She often felt depressed, and a deep, lonely sadness engulfed her. Her emotions seemed to sap all of the energy from her, leaving her exhausted. Several times she used the phrase, "I feel so lost; so helpless; so tired." Suddenly she interrupted her flow of words and asked with intense anger, "Why don't you people try and prepare people for this? I've always been able to control my emotions and move ahead. Now I feel helpless and hopeless."

After a pause, I said, "Before all of this happened, do you really think I could have described in words what you are feeling now? And if I could have done so, would you have believed me?"

The room became quiet as she thought about what I had said. The quiet stretched into minutes. Tears finally came, perhaps the first in a long time. Eventually she broke the silence. Shaking her head, she said softly, "No, I would never have believed that I could ever feel like I feel now. You are right. Nobody would believe it."

So, what do you do with the emotions you feel? How do you walk through the emotional storm?

YOUR EMOTIONS ARE NOT A SIGN OF WEAKNESS

Begin by affirming that your emotions are not wrong or a sign of weakness. Your emotions are a result of having lost someone you deeply loved. As has been said, your emotions are a tribute to that person. To try to reject your emotions or to feel that you are losing your mind is to misunderstand the healing process and to make light of the relationship you have had with the person you have lost.

Turn with me again to my analogy of the train wreck. If you had been in a physical train wreck and had been seriously injured, would you have felt embarrassed because you felt pain? In truth, the pain would be telling you what needed healing. You might not like what your body was telling you, but you would pay attention to it and accept it as part of the healing process.

So it is with the emotional train wreck of grief. You are feeling emotions you may never have felt before. Your tendency may be to try to deny them, reject them, or view them as a sign of weakness. But to reject your emotions is to postpone your healing.

Stages of Grief?

Years ago I held seminars on grief. I used a popular text that treated grief as occurring in steps or phases, orderly and predictable. One group I was teaching was made up of men who had suffered severe loss. The discussion one night turned into an analysis of which grief stage each man was in. Looking back, I cannot blame them because that is what I had taught them. But I knew something was amiss. They had become spectators of their grief. We cannot be spectators of our emotions any more than we can become spectators of our own major surgery.

When our family experienced our loss, we discovered right away that our emotions were unpredictable. They varied from one family member to another. While the stages of grief were truly identified, I seldom experienced my emotions in an orderly, predictable fashion. I remember thinking they were like a ball on a handball court, bouncing off all of the walls in every possible direction. Nor did they always progress from one stage to another. Some days I seemed to experience all of them in no predictable order. That is just the way it is with a loss that breaks your heart.

VALIDATE YOUR EMOTIONS

A better way to approach our emotions in grief is to acknowledge them, own them, and gently move into them instead of trying to analyze them. I like the phrase "validate your emotions." Legitimize them. Accept them. Confirm them. They are legitimate expressions of where you are emotionally and the loss you have experienced. More than that, they carry within them the healing circulation of grief. You see, the emotions of grief are a valid part of the healing process going on within you.

You may find that validating your emotions is not easy. It is as if you live in a foreign country, don't understand the language or the terrain, and wish you could somehow go back to where you were. But here you are, stuck in a place you do not want to be, with no ticket back to the way things were.

Putting Names on Emotions

So how do we validate our emotions and make them our own? In the myths and stories of the ancient world, there were often imaginary dragons, fearful beasts that destroyed everything. In the legends, taming those beasts was often begun by giving them a name.

One way that we can begin to live with our emotional dragons is to put names on them. The names you put on them may not be the names out of a book or the names I or someone else might give them. But look with me at a few of the more familiar names of the intense emotions that might come to live in our hearts.

THE DESPAIR OF IRREPLACEABLE LOSS

Kenneth Mitchell and Herbert Anderson mention the responses of men, some quite well known, as they experienced the loss of a spouse. A man called Jason felt part of him had died as well: "I feel that three quarters of me is gone forever." Congressman Claude Pepper reflected in a newspaper interview, "I am a ship without a rudder." C. S. Lewis wrote after the death of his wife that his body felt like an empty house.[1]

The most basic feeling in traumatic grief is loss. Nothing prepares us for feeling this way. Almost every experience in life repeats itself. We lose this game, but next season there is another. We are ill, but healing happens and we return to health. We are transferred to another job in another town and must leave our friends. In time, though, we make new friends and begin anew. But what do we do when the loss is final?

John Bramblett has written a moving story of his grief experience in his book *When Good-bye Is Forever: Learning to Live Again after the Loss of a Child.* He and his wife lost their little son Christopher in a tragic accident. Remembering those terrible moments after Christopher was killed, he wrote, "We cannot find words to convey the emptiness and pain that surge over us again and again."[2] A year later as he looked back to the passing of the weeks, which turned into months, he wrote, "The pain of our loss began to soften, but as it softened it also began to deepen. Reflecting on it now, we see that the softening comes from the distance that opens between us and the actual event of the death itself, and the deepening from the growing realization with each passing day that our child is truly gone from us—forever."[3]

Of course, there are many levels of emotional intensity. In contrast to the trauma about which John Bramblett wrote, other losses are not as devastating. When we lose older parents, for example, who may have been ill a long time, we feel the loss keenly. The grief is real. Sadness occurs. But in the midst of our loss we get on with our lives.

In contrast, the losses within a young family can be totally devastating. The loss comes to dominate every phase of life. Studies reveal that some of the greatest grief is that experienced by young widows. The future of their hopes and dreams is completely erased.

Dr. John Bowlby is an English author and psychotherapist. He studied cultures throughout the world, and he wrote a massive three-volume work, dividing life and relationships into three segments. Each volume bears the one-word title of that phase of life: *Attachment*, *Separation*, and *Loss*. *Loss* is the third volume.[4] I mention that volume because it reveals how significant a part of life loss is even if our modern culture largely ignores it.

SADNESS

As a result of the loss that we experience, a deep, lonely sadness takes residence within us.

All of us have known sadness before. To be human is to be sad sometimes. But there is a huge difference between our occasional setbacks and the deep, lonely sadness that comes when good-bye is forever. The intensity of this sadness will be different from one person to another. But a deep, lonely sadness will sooner or later set in.

A good friend I shall call Simon lost his wife some six years ago. They were inseparable. You will not talk with him very long until you realize how much he still walks with a lonely sadness. I asked him once, "What is the number one feeling that describes your grief?" Without hesitation he said, "Sadness. I have read books on grief, but I don't have what others have. I don't have great anger or depression or remorse. What I have is a deep sadness that never goes away. Sadness that she is gone and will never come back. And I miss her so."

A key feature of the sadness that comes from traumatic loss is that it moves in and stays around. In normal everyday living, a sad experience is usually replaced by a happy one. A down day is replaced by a better day. But the sadness that comes from irreplaceable loss doesn't catch the next train out of town. It moves in.

Does This Sadness Ever Go Away?

Many months, even years, after we lost Dave, I used to ask myself, *Does this sadness ever leave?* Not that I walked around with a long face anymore. My smile was back. But inside I still missed him so much. So it is a good question. Does this sadness last forever?

The answer is both yes and no.

First, let me answer yes. You will get over the sharp edges of your sadness. How? Let me draw you a mental picture, for I think in pictures when I can. One day I was reading an article about our physical hearts and how that muscle we call the heart needs space and nourishment, as well as protection. This is provided by a pericardial sac, a sac that surrounds the heart and allows it to move while still being protected and nourished. I said to myself, *That is the way it is with our broken hearts.*

Pretend (and this is an exercise in pretending) it is like that with your emotionally broken heart. Imagine that your broken heart is contained in an invisible pericardial sac that began to grow when your unthinkable loss happened. Picture it growing slowly, ever so slowly. Eventually, perhaps years later, it completely contains and protects your broken heart with all of its memories, its feelings, and its loss. It also contains and isolates your sadness. The horizons of your life are no longer all about your loss. You are allowed to once again embrace your purpose in life, your work, your family life, your recreation, and your faith. In this sense, yes, you get over your sadness. You live much of your life without the sadness that in earlier days seemed always there because of your loss. Your memories are protected, even nourished, in that invisible pericardial sac.

Now, let me answer no. It is also true that you never get completely over your sadness because of the loss you have experienced. That imaginary pericardial sac is quite thin. All it takes is a picture, a memory, a song, or an anniversary, and you feel the sadness of the loss all over again. But would you want it any other way? Would you really like to never again remember the one you loved so much? I don't think so. The way to turn these sad times into positive times is to remember and be thankful.

Once again the wisdom of grief has arranged for us to get on with our lives while at the same time allowing us to keep touch with the precious memories we don't want to lose. To use that imaginary picture again, those precious memories are preserved and protected by the invisible pericardial sac that is around your broken heart.

FEAR

Fear is an emotion with which we are acquainted. But few of us ever thought about having to live with intense fear as part of grief. We fear what the future holds. We fear what might happen next. We fear that we will never get over the loss and sadness that we feel. It may be helpful to know that C. S. Lewis, after the death of his wife, wrote in the opening words of *A Grief Observed,* "No one ever told me that grief felt so much like fear."[5]

When Tom Crider lost his only child, twenty-one-year-old Gretchen, in an apartment fire, he wrote of his anguish, sometimes using the pronoun *I,* other times, the pronoun *he:*

> *I walk through the valley of the shadow of death, but, unlike the psalmist, I fear evil everywhere.*
>
> It's deeper than fear, really, it's dread. . . . When the phone rings his heart bounds. He thinks someone else has died: Mieke, his mother, his brother, a friend. . . . Everything it meant to be a father is gone, suddenly and forever.[6]

Fear paralyzes our trust, our attitudes, our optimism. Fear buries itself so deeply into the soul of grief that it can become a major cause of depression. God takes our fears most seriously. The early words of the angels to the shepherds at the birth of Jesus were these: "Fear not: for, behold, I bring you good tidings of great joy, which shall be to all people" (Luke 2:10 KJV).

The antidote to fear is trust. But trust is hard to come by in heartbreaking loss. Fear is replaced by trust, piece by piece and brick by brick. Some never get there. Bitterness sets in and stays. But bitterness is a high price to pay for rejecting the relearning of trust. Replacing fear with trust will take time. It will mean opening yourself to a power beyond yourself. Proverbs 3:5-6 has been a stabilizer for so many in the midst of grief:

Trust in the LORD with all your heart
and lean not on your own understanding;
in all your ways acknowledge him,
and he will make your paths straight. (NIV)

ANGER

Anger is another significant part of loss. In some ways it penetrates almost every part of the grief experience. We are angry that it happened. We are angry that we live in a world in which it could happen. We are angry at God for allowing it to happen. We are angry that things can never again be what once they were because it happened.

Anger will surface. You may think you have locked it in the basement of your soul. But it has the key to the lock. It will let its fury out at unpredictable times.

Gardening is one of my hobbies. It was also a way to get away from things during the years following Dave's death. One spring day I was chopping weeds with a hoe. Suddenly, without warning, I began hitting that hoe against the ground as hard as I could. As I did, I began to cry. It was obvious what was happening. My psyche gave the anger from the pent-up grief experience permission to get out. Did it ever! Nothing like that had ever happened to me before. My pent-up anger was surfacing as I was banging my hoe against the ground. Deep within I felt betrayed because of the unfairness of it all. Why did Dave die? He wanted to live so badly. Why not the guy down the hall who had leukemia? He was an avowed atheist with a terrible attitude. His cynical demeanor often surfaced in his declaration that he really didn't care if he lived or died. He lived, but Dave died. It seemed so unfair. My anger was coming out through that hoe.

On that day in the garden I was beating that hoe against the ground with such force that the handle broke! I sat down and sobbed and cried as I had not cried in many years, maybe never. But I discovered in that experience a huge draining of anger that was a major step toward healing. I broke several hoe handles that spring!

Breaking a hoe handle is not likely to be your answer. My judgment is that you will bump into something that will serve as an emotional outlet where you can deposit your intense emotions safely. Most important, you must not take out your anger on someone else!

In the Bible, some of the most faithful individuals took out their anger on God. The prophet Jeremiah, for example, was put in the stocks at the city gate so people could laugh and make fun of him. When he was released, he vented his anger at God (Jer. 20:7-18). His anger explosion began, "O LORD, you deceived me, and I was deceived" (NIV). If you need to explode to somebody, consider taking it out on God, like Jeremiah did. After all, God has heard it all before. Besides, God already knows it's there.

GUILT

Sooner or later you are likely to play the "if only" game. "If only" we had done thus and so, this would not have happened.

"If only" we had *not* done this, the outcome would have been different. Sometimes we put the blame on ourselves. Other times we put the blame on someone else. In either case we are dealing with a huge harvest of guilt.

The "if only" game is especially prevalent in accidents: "If I had been there, this would not have happened," or "Why wasn't so-and-so able to prevent this?" The "if only" game is particularly likely for those of us who have spent much of our lives in charge of things—in charge of the family, in charge of the business, in charge of the classroom, or in charge of nurturing and caring for others. We feel terribly guilty because we couldn't take charge and keep the tragedy from happening. This "if only" game gathers momentum when we second-guess treatment options. With cancer we sometimes say, "If only we had chosen this treatment or protocol instead of the one we chose."

Also, it is a huge temptation to change the "if only" game into the "blame" game. Sometimes there are those who could be blamed for what happened. But in the end, both the "if only" game and the "blame" game turn their backs on the future and concentrate totally on the past.

From "If Only" to "Now Then"

When the "if only" game has taken up long-term residence in your mind and heart, consider this change in attitude and perspective. *Change from "if only" to "now then."* You cannot change what has been. Although you may not be able to forget it, you can begin to fasten your attention on what can be. Sometime in the months or even years following your loss, the wisdom of grief may begin to whisper in the ears of your broken heart, "Turn your attention from 'if only' to 'now then.'" It will not happen at once, but eventually your horizons will begin to change. The wisdom of grief will prompt you to say, "If I could change what happened, I would do it in a heartbeat, but I can't. I must accept what can't be changed. *Now then*, where do I go from here?"

TEARS

Another way in which you can gain some relief from your anxiety, your anger, and your guilt is through tears.

Tears are part of us from our earliest days and may become an essential part of your healing. You must cease to be embarrassed when tears come. Tears surface in grief, often in times of fatigue and exhaustion. Dr. Daniel Bagby says, "The weary soul weeps tears that bathe its worn-out soil."[7]

Tears are not emotions, yet they are often a true mirror of your emotions. Dr. Bagby speaks of the "vocabulary of our tears" and reflects on the understanding that they bring to us: "To understand ourselves, we must understand our tears."[8] In special ways during grief, tears are the vocabulary of your broken dreams, and they mirror the pain of your irrevocable loss.

In the moments of sudden sorrow you may, in shock, be tearless. But later, when you truly begin to realize what has happened, tears flow. They become the vocabulary of your sorrow and speak a language that you and others will understand. In the wisdom of grief, tears bring forth healing moments.

ACCEPTING THE EMOTIONAL TERRAIN

You must accept that grief is an emotional journey. It is not a comfortable walk for any of us. You are in unfamiliar emotional territory. The air you breathe is the sadness that you feel. Angry eruptions happen inside you, which you hesitate to own. Despair and even depression can become part of the horizon. Fear lingers through it all.

You must also accept that within these emotional upheavals, grief is doing its work. The quickest way to achieve some kind of normalcy is to accept these emotions as healing avenues. They won't feel like it. They may feel just the opposite. But remember to own and affirm your emotions, for they are legitimate. They are often the healing ways that grief uses to bring about the healing of loss.

****

This I Can Do Today:

I can begin to accept my emotions as legitimate expressions of my loss and grief.

This I Can Remember Today:

I can remember the image of an invisible pericardial sac around my broken heart that keeps my memories secure and safe but allows me to get on with my life.

CHAPTER FOUR

Decide Whom to Talk To

Our culture does not have much empathy or sympathy for the emotions of grief. We grow up with the notion that to show one's grieving emotions is a sure sign of weakness and a suggestion that the person is completely out of control. This notion is truly hypocritical. For it is quite acceptable for others to show emotions at a game or a concert, even to the point of being wildly out of control. But to show grieving emotions in public is a sure sign that a person is emotionally sick and even neurotic. Herbert Anderson and Kenneth Mitchell state: "To admit one's grief verbally, much less to show it in one's face or body, is often taken as a sign of loss of self control." They then put their finger on the negative significance of this when it comes to the healing of heartbreaking grief: "This need for control is a serious impediment to successful resolution of grief."[1]

Those of us who are grieving are caught in a real trap. On the one hand, the healing of grief requires our willingness to express our emotions—to let them surface and in so doing to bring about a measure of healing. On the other hand, if we let these emotions surface in public, especially to the point of anger or tears, we will be immediately labeled as emotionally disturbed. For example, C. S. Lewis wrote in *A Grief Observed* concerning his insecurity at this point: "An odd by-product of my loss is that I'm aware of being an embarrassment to everyone I meet. . . . Perhaps the bereaved ought to be isolated in special settlements like lepers."[2] No one who is working through grief wants to be labeled, especially if the label implies emotional weakness. But *not* to share the feelings of our grief is to risk deep depression. So what do we do?

A PERSONAL ABOUT-FACE

In one of her books, author Carol S. Pearson wrote of a friend for whom the real heroes in life are those who, no matter how much suffering they experience, do not pass it on to others. They absorb it and declare, "The suffering stops here."[3] I remember giving an affirming nod many years ago when I read that. Most of us have no need to inflict our troubles on someone else. I determined that I would be that kind of hero. Whatever happened, I would say with courage and determination, "The suffering stops here."

Now, having walked through major grief with others and having experienced heartbreaking grief myself, I would disagree. "The suffering stops here" may work in many instances. But when grief breaks your heart, it is much too heavy for you to declare, "The suffering stops here." No matter how strong you are, in heavy grief the issue is not *Where does the suffering stop?* but *With whom will I share my grief?*

TWO EXTREMES

Consider the approaches of people I have known. A woman I will call Mary enjoys talking. Some would claim she has never had an unspoken thought. When unthinkable grief broke in upon her life, she continued her habit of talking. She shared her inner anguish with everyone. Even strangers got a full load of her distress and grief. With Mary the suffering stopped nowhere and was spread everywhere. Unfortunately, Mary is slowly but surely causing isolation. People are withdrawing from her. They cannot handle her continual distress. More than ever before she needs others, and she is doing the very thing that drives them away. Clearly, to act as if the suffering stops nowhere is not a good answer.

A man I will call Andy is the opposite of Mary. Ask Andy a question and he will process it for two weeks and then come to you with a brief answer. By then you have forgotten the question! Now that traumatic loss has entered Andy's life, his natural and normal tendency is to process everything by himself. He is not comfortable sharing with anyone. But little by little he is ceasing to function. As he continues to process everything within, his sorrow is grinding him up inside. He has grown even quieter. He has quit eating regularly. He has trouble sleeping. He is withdrawing from everyone.

Andy's friends are worried about him. His attempt to keep his suffering to himself isn't working. His friends are deeply concerned. They try to break into his solitude by calling him and even dropping by to see him. All of this is to no avail. They fear that unless Andy can begin to break out of his isolation, his unresolved grief is apt to have severe physical and emotional consequences. Clearly, handling his deep sorrow all by himself is not a singular experience, even if Andy wants it to be.

OUR TIME TO CHOOSE

Now let's talk about you and me. We would do well to avoid both extremes, talking to everyone or talking to no one. We need to talk to someone who has been where we have been, or who has counseled with people who are where we are.

Choosing someone to talk to will not be easy. Inertia is apt to whisper, "You are just having a down day. You can do this all by yourself." Or the postponement gremlin might whisper, "You need to do this but put it off until you feel better. You wouldn't want anyone to see you like this." You listen to the gremlin, and as the days go by, everything is drifting lower.

Accept this truth about yourself. If you felt this bad because of something physical, you would have long since sought help. But emotions? You think you can handle emotional distress by yourself.

What you will need to do as you seek help is to keep your decisions and your appointments to yourself. How does the old saying go? "Be wise as serpents and innocent as doves" (Matt. 10:16b). You will find you can do that surprisingly well. I think the reason is that you know you are handling things with your friend or your counselor and it is a secret between the two of you.

WARNING SIGNS

What are some warning signs suggesting that you need to seek a person or two with whom you can talk?

- If others are withdrawing from you, you are talking too much. You need to find someone with whom you can share. The suffering stops there.
- If you are trying to handle things all by yourself, you are apt to become dysfunctional and depressed.
- If you can't sleep at night.
- If your emotions, such as anger, surface at inappropriate times.
- If you weep at almost anything and everything.
- If you give in to the tendency to isolate yourself from everyone.
- If you despair about your life and the future.

THREE SPECIFIC EMOTIONAL SIGNALS

Perhaps the list above doesn't speak to your situation. Take your temperature—your emotional temperature—with three measurements.

Loneliness

A sense of being alone can settle on your broken heart even with others all around you. Grief is an individual matter. Members of the family and closest friends are not apt to handle grief the same way you feel it. This loneliness is not something you would like to talk to them about. But it has taken over a corner of your being and doesn't seem to want to move on. Left alone, loneliness has a way of turning into despair and then into depression.

When loneliness has become the environment of your heart and soul, it is time to talk to someone. There is an old German proverb that says, "Don't go too far all alone."

Sleeplessness

The inability to sleep is also part of the emotional family of isolation. Unfortunately, however much you want to go to sleep, wanting to go to sleep doesn't help. You cannot will yourself to sleep. Instead you wander about in the forest of your fears, worrying about everything under the sun. Because sleep comes in little bits and pieces, a constant sense of tiredness sets in. It is time to see someone, even if it is your family physician. The physician may give you something that will help you sleep. As mine said to me, "You've got to start getting some sleep, or you are going nowhere but down."

Emptiness

Your sense of loss has moved into the rooms of your heart, and a deep emptiness has set in. The emptiness grows as you realize how final everything is. An empty hole is left in your heart because the one you have lost is truly gone. There is no one to take that person's place. This is as it should be. No one can take his or her place. Eventually you will accept and get used to this void. But in the meantime, your emotional emptiness often makes you feel that you are walking this journey alone. You are not, of course. But it is time to reach out to someone you can talk to.

Review these signals. Does one or more look familiar? Then it is time to take initiative and find someone with whom to share your journey.

OPTION ONE:
A FRIEND WHO HAS BEEN THERE

Dr. Charles Brown is a professor in pastoral care at Union Theological Seminary. Charlie has taught more pastors than anyone I know about grief and about how to help parishioners with grief. His deep conviction is that a person who has suffered heartbreaking grief is going to need professional help to get through it. From my experience, I would agree. But I also know of rare instances when a person has relied upon a friend for counseling and support. It would be a rare friend who could do this. But it is possible.

Ann Kaiser Stearns relates the experience of a friend named Hope. She was trying to gain her equilibrium after a tragedy. "How do you do this?" Hope asked a close friend. She knew her friend would understand where she was, because her son had been killed eight years earlier in a mountain climbing accident three days before he was to graduate from medical school. In addition, three years later her friend had lost her husband to cancer.

Hope was in the midst of the deepest despair of her life. "How do you do this? We're not sure we can live to the next day." Her friend, who knew that easy answers wouldn't suffice, thought for a moment and then said softly, "I don't know how I did it, but here I am."[4] Hope did not need an easy, superficial answer to the agony she was feeling. She needed a friend who had been there, someone to talk to. Presence was probably as important, maybe more important, as counsel or advice.

If you can find such a friend, that may be your answer. But this person should meet three qualifications. First, he or she needs to have gone through what you are going through. If not, this person has no idea where you are. Second, this person needs to be able to listen and handle tears and silence, for a lot of both go into this kind of sharing. Third, this person needs to absolutely keep confidences.

OPTION TWO: A COUNSELOR WHO IS A GOOD FIT

My experience may be of help as you consider this option. There came a point in my grief journey when I had become almost dysfunctional. Early on I had decided to handle the suffering privately. "The suffering stops here," I had told myself. Of course, it was deceitful. My inner pain was so great and so obvious that anyone around me could pick it up. I wasn't handling my suffering by myself at all. Like Andy above, I was just fooling myself. Even worse, there were times when I couldn't keep my sorrow within myself and tears came. Even my best friends could not handle my emotion.

So I made the decision to share the journey with a psychiatrist. I went to one, but it was not a good fit. I went to another, and it was even worse. Then I sought the advice of one of my parishioners who was a counselor. She shook her head. "Who pastors the pastor?" she asked. "I can't think of anyone." I gave up. I shuffled through my days as best I could, but there was no life, much less joy, in that journey.

One day I received a letter from that parishioner who was a counselor. She wrote to say she had thought and prayed about my request to have someone to talk to. In her letter she gave me the name of a man I did not know, but she described him as "the smartest and wisest man I know." I knew sometime during the first visit that it was a good fit, a wise choice. He became my Moses, who walked with me through the desert of heartbreaking grief into a new land of promise. It took a long time. But with his help I— better, we—made it. Yet in a short time I was able to say to myself, "My suffering is going to stop in his office." And it did.

In addition, my wife, Shirley, was further along in the grief process than I was. We are different personalities, and we handled our grief in different ways. We read that divorce was often the result when a married couple suffered severe, unexpected trauma. We didn't want that to happen. We were advised to share with different counselors. We did, and that worked for us. She with hers; I with mine.

Let me share a mistake I made, with the thought that you might avoid it. On occasion, I broke my rule of sharing only with my counselor. Sometimes I would be with close friends who lived in other cities. When we were together, usually at a meeting, they were good enough to ask how I was doing. I tried to answer as faithfully and as honestly as possible. Doing that was a huge mistake, though. Sometimes they handled it well, but most of the time they could not handle the intensity of my grief. One spoke to my wife and asked, "Is Jim like this all the time?" In my naïveté I thought I was just answering his question, "How are you doing?" Looking back, I think he was just extending a greeting like, "How are ya?" I learned to let the pain, anger, and despair that I felt at the death of my son stop in the office of the counselor.

WHAT ABOUT SHARING WITH GOD?

Add one more dimension. Take your despair, your anger, even your doubt, to God. Let God absorb some of the outrage that you feel. Having been there before with countless others, God can handle it. Besides, the Lord already knows about it. God is the one before whom no secrets are hid. You may be as mad as hell at God, but heaven can handle it. The book of Psalms is full of such outbursts. Read through the Psalms and you will be surprised at how many express your thoughts and feelings exactly.

A critical question about your emotional suffering is this: Where will the suffering stop? Don't try to handle it with everyone. Don't try to handle it all by yourself. The real hero is one who shares suffering not with everybody, or alone, but handles it with one or two others and with God.

****

This I Can Do Today:

I need to share with only one or two persons and with God.

This I Can Remember Today:

I can remember the old German proverb: "Don't go too far all alone."

CHAPTER FIVE

When One Day at a Time Is Too Much

The wise men and women of the ages have said, "Take one day at a time." It is wonderful advice to normal worried and anxious people in a normal worried and anxious world. In truth, most people would be so much better off if they could put their anxieties about the future on the shelf and take one day at a time. Jesus said, "Do not worry about tomorrow, for tomorrow will worry about itself. Each day has enough trouble of its own" (Matt. 6:34 NIV). Taking one day at a time is a helpful, if difficult, discipline during normal times. However, *we are not in a normal time!*

Dr. Gerald Mann is the author of the book *When One Day at a Time Is Too Long*. The provocative title happened like this: Gerald and his wife, Lois, were sitting in a restaurant some years ago, reviewing the life they had lived together. Tragedies had been part of their journey. One was an accident for which they were not responsible, but it took the lives of some fine young military men who had run a stop sign at an open country intersection. Dr. Mann was a hugely successful pastor, and their conversation inevitably came around to how they had survived all of this. Lois boiled it down to taking one day at a time. Dr. Mann blurted out, "Bull! One day at a time was too damned long." He explained in his book that he had never heard it or said it before. It was one of those phrases that "thought me up." Then he came to realize how much of his life had been spent "connecting with those for whom one day at a time is too long . . . people who are hurting so much that they need hope to make it from moment to moment."[1]

When heartbreaking loss is ours, at least sometime during our grief walk, one day at a time is just too much. In her book *Widow* Lynn Caine wrote of the days when her loss overtook her:

> When the protective fog of numbness had finally dissipated, life became truly terrifying. I was full of grief, choked with unshed tears, overwhelmed by the responsibility of bringing up two children alone, panicked about my financial situation, almost immobilized by the stomach-wrenching, head-splitting pain of realizing that I was alone. My psychic pain was such that putting a load of dirty clothes in the washing machine, taking out the vacuum cleaner, making up a grocery list, all the utterly routine household chores, loomed like Herculean labors.[2]

What do we do when one day at a time is too much?

Let's begin with an honest look at how our world trains us to solve our problems lest we get down on ourselves and think we are weak and even losing our minds.

WHY DO WE FEEL WEAK
AND HELPLESS?

Why is it that we, who have functioned well throughout all of our lives, can't handle what is happening now? Here is a large part of the answer. The ways in which you and I have always managed our lives, usually successfully, are virtually useless when we are suddenly forced to handle heavy grief. Consider some things that worked for us during normal times but are not able to help us much, if at all, in heartbreaking loss.

"Fix It" Won't Work

Often in our lives we play the role of Doctor Fix It. A child falls and scrapes the skin, calling for a bandage. We get that bandage, lovingly place it on the wound, and say, "There, that ought to fix it." On a deeper level, when relationships are strained in family or among friends, we try to fix it. At work, when performance is down and improvements are needed, we try to fix it. Sometimes we discover there are parts of our lives that need fixing. Our first attempt is usually to fix it ourselves.

But when we lose someone in heartbreaking grief, there is nothing we can do to fix anything. Others will try to help us fix it. Though they mean well, they have never been where we are, or they would know that fixing things is impossible. We cannot bring back the one we have lost. We cannot fix how it happened. We cannot erase the implications of what has happened. The truth is, we cannot fix anything about our loss. No wonder we feel lost and helpless.

"Figure It Out and Think It Through" Doesn't Work

In ordinary life when things seem out of control, we put our minds to figure it out and think it through. Often we do. We have had lots of practice. Even in preschool we begin figuring things out. It continues as a mainstream of modern life. It is the outcome of a society that has bought hook, line, and sinker the key thought of the philosopher Descartes: "I think, therefore I am." The insinuation is that if I can think through a challenge, everything will be fine. A successful person correctly analyzes, evaluates, makes adjustments, and proceeds. More often than not, success happens.

There is nothing wrong with this thinking for certain parts of our lives. In fact, one form of therapy these days is cognitive therapy, which is a more sophisticated version of the power of positive thinking. In normal life situations, even mild depression, this can work. It can even change our attitudes about life. But it is virtually useless when our lives have been devastated by the emotional and relational loss of someone whom we have loved so much and who is now gone forever. In our situation, trying to figure things out and think things through is like trying to remove a mountain with a shovel.

"Willpower and Want to" Don't Work

Another way we navigate through life is with willpower. As coaches say, "It is all about want to." We picture the will as the great shaker and mover in making a path for the way that we want life to go. But we never would have chosen life to take the turn that it has.

Let me quickly affirm that during normal times, we *are* able to move forward because we really want to. We do set things in motion with our willpower. But in the wounding and devastation of heartbreaking grief, when everything seems to be blown apart, we cannot will what *was* back into existence. We cannot will that our grief will go away. We cannot will away the inner pain. We cannot will the person we have lost back into being.

In truth, willpower is helpless in many life situations. We can't will ourselves to sleep. We can't will contentment or peace of mind. No matter how much we want to, we cannot relive what has been. We cannot will for another person a change of life-style that will take him or her out of addiction. We cannot make another person love us, no matter how much we want him or her to. Most of all, in a grief-bound situation, willpower will not heal a broken heart. It will not bring back the one who is gone. It will not build a bridge between what has been and what can be. That bridge will be built one small, healing brick at a time as grief turns from being a center of loss to becoming a healing center for the future.

WHAT DO WE DO RIGHT NOW?

So, in the midst of being almost totally overcome by grief, what do we do just to get through the next part of the day?

Take Small Steps

I believe I could return to the very spot where it happened. It was for me a moment of deep, demobilizing grief, of emotional, mental, and physical exhaustion. It happened sometime during the second year after we had lost our son. On my way to make a pastoral visit to a person in the hospital, I was walking down a hospital hall with rooms on both sides, doors closed. I stopped, frozen in my tracks, and leaned against the wall. I just couldn't go on. Fortunately no one was coming or going. I stood there a few minutes saying to myself, *I cannot go on. How can I be of help to someone who is sick when I am in the shape I am in?* I couldn't move. In that helpless moment I felt the word come to me from within, *Just take the next step. Then take the next one. Walk through the rest of the day, one step at a time.*

I believe that was a helpful word from the Lord. One step at a time I walked into that room and was able to be an encourager in a difficult situation. It was an amazing moment for me. It was as if I was an exhausted, drained, empty shell through whom encouraging words were passing. I was simply being used to help because I had no strength or power in and of myself. As I left the hospital and walked to the parking deck, I realized that the Lord had taught me a crucial, basic lesson: when one day at a time is too much, take one step at a time. In the next days and weeks it became my mantra for every day: just take one step at a time. When one day at a time is too much, shrink things down to just taking the next step.

You may have had practice in your work or profession at trimming a single day down to little segments for the sake of planning and time management. Perhaps you can use that discipline to trim your day into little pieces just to get through it. I read recently about a successful basketball coach who instructs his team to play a game in four-minute segments. He has come to realize a full game is too much.

We need to have the determination to keep going, to take one step at a time into what we know we ought to be doing. Keep saying to yourself, *Somehow I will make it. God, help me take one more step.*

Do Something Rather than Nothing

Remember this: *Taking the next step is still moving forward. Taking the next step is choosing to do something rather than nothing.* Healing happens anytime a person in a traumatic situation chooses to do something small but positive, to do something instead of nothing.

At Bethlehem, in a stable and in a manger, Jesus was born. It happened virtually unnoticed. No press corps. No national leaders. No religious leaders. No bishops. No city dignitaries. To be sure, eventually the shepherds came. But shepherds were on the lowest rung of the vocational ladder. Nobody grew up wanting to be a shepherd! What was really happening was God doing the next thing! It was God doing something instead of nothing! Look at the result! There is always healing in moving forward, doing something, however small and seemingly insignificant.

Right now, turn quietly, and lean into your sadness. Then, one step at a time, do something instead of nothing.

****

This I Can Do Today:

I can take the next step. I can keep putting one foot in front of the other.

This I Can Remember Today:

I can remember that when one day is too much, doing something is better than doing nothing.

CHAPTER SIX

Find Your Releasing Activities

WHAT WINSTON CHURCHILL DISCOVERED

Once during a particularly painful grief time, I remembered something I had read years ago concerning Winston Churchill and World War II. Churchill, you may remember, was the prime minister of England during the Second World War. The immense loss of life and property resulting from the Battle of Britain almost brought the British under Nazi domination. Churchill's positive courage during those awful days was part of what turned the tide for the English and ultimately for the war. How did Churchill hold himself together in the darkest days of loss?

He provided an answer in his little book titled *Painting as a Pastime*. Churchill handled stress by losing himself in his painting.

Painting? Yes, Churchill was a painter—the kind of painter who paints on canvas. He embraced painting not so much by training as by necessity. In trying to find something that would distract his mind from the pressures he felt, he bumped into the power of picking up a brush and painting on a canvas. It had the capacity to tear his mind away from the trauma he was going through and, for a time, focus his mind on what he was painting. His little book tells his story. I quote his first three paragraphs:

> Many remedies are suggested for the avoidance of worry and mental overstrain. . . . Some recommend exercise, and others, repose. Some counsel travel, and others, retreat. Some praise solitude, and others, gaiety. No doubt all these may play their part according to the individual temperament. But the element which is constant and common in all of them is Change.
>
> Change is the master key. . . . It is not enough merely to switch off the lights which play upon the main and ordinary field of interest; a new field of interest must be illuminated. It is no use saying to the tired "mental muscles"—if one may coin such an expression—"I will give you a good rest," "I will go for a long walk," or "I will lie down and think of nothing." The mind keeps busy just the same. If it has been weighing and measuring, it goes on weighing and measuring. If it has been worrying, it goes on worrying. It is only when new cells are called into activity, when new stars become the lords of the ascendant, that relief, repose, refreshment are afforded.
>
> A gifted American psychologist has said, "Worry is a spasm of the emotion; the mind catches hold of something and will not let it go." It is useless to argue with the mind in this condition. The stronger the will, the more futile the task. One can only gently insinuate something else into its convulsive grasp. And if this something else is rightly chosen, if it is really attended by the illumination of another field of interest, gradually, and often

quite swiftly, the old undue grip relaxes and the process of re-cuperation and repair begins.[1]

For Churchill, this release, this distraction, came from paint-ing. Golf did not seem to hold his interest. Exercise may have been good for his body but did nothing to release the grip that stress had on his mind. In painting on a canvas he found his answer.

The wisdom of grief is apt to point you toward finding some releasing or distracting activity that will ease your loss-bound mind for a while. During my journey through such treacherous times, it seemed that the power of loss grabbed my mind and would not let go. Some-times it felt like a treble fish hook, a hook with three sharp points, digging into my mind from all directions. Try as I might, I could not dislodge the overwhelming feeling of loss and of the unfairness of it all. My appetite suffered. A good night's sleep became an exception.

One feature of the wisdom of grief is that parts of the mind *have not been wounded by the experiences we have been through.* We feel that we are wounded all over. The pain and sorrow are so over-whelming in the one part of our souls that it seems to be the only part. We need to discover the areas that are still whole and healthy. When we do, the traumatized parts of us rest for a while.

THE DISCOVERY OF A RELEASING ACTIVITY

What is the releasing, or distracting, activity for you? You need to claim or discover it. It might be a hobby you enjoyed in previous days. It might be some new endeavor. The test is this: *Can you lose yourself in it?* It needs to be powerful enough that the treble hook of loss, which is lodged in your mind, will finally let loose, giving your loss-bound mind a rest.

When I unearthed Churchill's principle of distraction, I was immediately convinced that he was right on target. I needed something that was engaging enough to allow my grief-filled mind a rest. Ordinarily I would turn immediately to prayer. Prayer is for me a constant relationship and communication with God. Many of my prayers during this time were protests, such as those in the Psalms. But my prayers were often centered on my grief and family and church needs. I needed something so different that it would give my traumatized mind a rest. I interviewed others and experimented with my possibilities of releasing areas. Here are some of them.

Put Feelings on Paper

Julia Cameron is into renewal, helping people find their way in life or, more often, find their way back from difficult times in life. She holds seminars to assist people in this regard. The substance of these is to be found in two of her books, *The Artist's Way*[2] and *The Vein of Gold*.[3] In both she writes about, and in her seminars requires, what she calls "morning pages."

Morning pages are three pages to be written every morning on three regular notebook pages. The participant is to write on these pages whatever "stuff" comes to mind. No thought is to be given to content, grammar, spelling, or whatever. It is to get the "stuff" of the soul out of the head and heart and onto the paper. In so doing, the writer of the morning pages is able to enter the day without all of the clutter that ordinarily is carried into the day's work. Also, it is to be written by hand rather than on a computer. Something about writing words longhand seems to help us access the troubles of the heart more easily than using a computer does. My wife, Shirley, did practice and continues to practice this activity. She suggested that I try it. What did I have to lose?

I decided to try the morning page routine when the emotions of my grief were almost unmanageable. Frankly, it was like a survival mechanism; it worked for me. I still do morning pages when the stress surfaces or I am confronting something I can't dislodge from my mind. I made two changes to Cameron's routine, both of which worked well for me. First, I focused on emotions, not simply on the stuff that might be ahead for that day. Writing as fast as I could, often virtually illegibly, I would pour out my emotions, whatever they were, onto the page, giving no thought to grammar, spelling, or appropriateness. Second, so that I could be completely honest with what I was feeling and writing, I would tear those pages up after I finished them. I never had to worry about anybody reading them, which allowed me to put down on paper exactly what I was feeling and how it was affecting me. It was like throwing my most intense emotions in the trash basket before I started the day.

For some, a journal is preferable to morning pages. When C. S. Lewis lost his wife to cancer, he kept a journal. Of course, he was a renowned writer. For him, journaling became a healing time. It was release. It was a way of getting rid of some small part of the pain. Madeleine L'Engle said it well in her foreword to the Lewis classic *A Grief Observed*: "It is all right to wallow in one's journal;

it is a way of getting rid of self-pity and self-indulgence and self-centeredness. What we work out in our journals we don't take out on family and friends."[4]

Beauty

Sometimes people find what releases the grief-bound mind almost by accident. This happened to Mary Jane Worden. She and her husband, Jim, were staff members of Inter-Varsity Christian Fellowship until his tragic death in a car accident. She tells about the traumatic journey of grief for her and her three children in her book *Early Widow*. It was for her, as it is for all of us, a torturous journey full of pain, of loss, of ups and downs. Six months after Jim's death, she wrote in a letter to friends, "I am still occasionally swept by . . . the staggering awareness that Jim is not, and never will be, with us here again. But I'm learning that the best way to get to the other side is to go through it, to face it and to name it."[5]

One day she began to sense a pattern working within her that gave her some release from the grief and loss. She wrote, "The principle is this: beauty can help to bring healing—rainbows, mountains, woolly lambs, fresh strawberries on homemade ice cream, the crisp clean feel of sun-dried sheets. These places and things were somehow soothing to my soul."[6]

Another widow shared with me that when she is in church and cannot keep her mind on the worship, she has learned to fasten her attention on the flowers. The flowers, she said, have a way of turning her attention away from her loss, and a sense of calmness returns. She is then able to give her attention once more to the worship of God.

Gardening

Gardening is for many a way to lose themselves and their grief for a while. It is a combination of losing themselves in the present and investing themselves in the future. Both are essential during a grief time.

In addition, most gardeners find something therapeutic about getting in the soil and getting their hands dirty. One of my good friends of yesteryear was Shaw Cunningham. He was a dedicated gardener well into his eighties. On occasion I would find him in his garden with his wife, Lillian, looking on as he would point to a garden plaque prominently displayed:

> The kiss of the sun for pardon,
> The song of the birds for mirth,
> One is nearer God's heart in a garden,
> Than anywhere else on earth.
> (*The Lord God Planted a Garden*, by Dorothy Gurney)

Then with a smile on his face and a twinkle in his eye, he would churn a bit of his earthbound theology by saying, "Remember, God was a gardener before he was anything else."

For others, gardening is sheer escape. When I asked one woman who had suffered heartbreaking loss about how she managed her way through it, she answered, "I discovered I could lose myself in my garden."

The Hand Connection

Sometimes the releasing activity is related to what a person does with his or her hands. Something about creating with one's hands seems to release one's grief mind for a while. As a by-product, the person may be creating beautiful things or beautiful places.

A man I know has discovered release by working with wood. He and his wife had moved to a retirement center and were exceedingly happy there. Then she became ill and was gone before either would have imagined. Sixty years of marriage abruptly ended. The loss of his wife left a gaping hole in his life. His friends both within and outside the retirement center were deeply concerned about him. He seemed totally lost without her. As time went on, he seemed to sense that he needed something to lose himself in. The retirement center had a woodworking shop. He remembered enjoying shop classes long ago in school. First, he observed. Then, he asked questions. Some participants had walked the same road he was walking and welcomed him. As he began to work with his hands, he gained some release from his sorrow.

Part of the releasing seems to happen with creating beauty with the hands. Several women I know, including my wife, Shirley, are potters. Working with clay, either using the wheel or hand-building, allows them to put aside for a time the severe losses they have experienced. In creating something beautiful with their hands, their hearts are healed. Creating seems to have within its creative power the possibility of rekindling life and hope. Most of all it allows the grief mind some space to rest.

Music

I knew my releasing activity, unlike Winston Churchill's, was not painting. When I was in the third grade, the art teacher gave up on me! Nor am I a craftsman, like one who carves or works with wood, or who shapes and molds clay.

What about athletics, such as golf or tennis? I was not a good golfer but had enjoyed it in former days. But in some ways, the frustrations of my golf game added to, rather than detracted from, the emotions I was trying to leave behind. As for tennis, my optometrist tells me that my eyes turn outward when a moving ball approaches. Some of my best friends are runners. They claim that in their distance running, marathons and the like, they literally lose themselves, concentrating on keeping their time and pace, and sometimes trying to compete with others. But I am not a runner.

Then, one day, almost by accident, I sat down at the piano and began to play. I hadn't played seriously, often not at all, for many years. I had in fact gone to college to major in piano and organ. My football scholarship and my decision to enter the ministry put all of that on the shelf. I wasn't very good at it after all of those years, but that was good in itself. It took my total concentration. Eventually it began to return to me. The great thing about it was that I could lose myself completely in it. I could not paint like Churchill, but maybe he couldn't play the piano either!

Another Kind of Reading

If you ever walk through an airport waiting area, you are apt to find people reading—often novels. During the summer at the beach, I am always surprised and amused at how many are under a beach umbrella reading.

I love to read and began to wonder whether this might be a diversion or releasing activity for me. It became an answer at bedtime because I was having great trouble sleeping. I needed something light but intriguing that would deactivate my grief mind so I could get some rest. I discovered the mystery novels of Tony Hillerman. The mysteries are cast within the culture and ways of the Navajo of the American Southwest. The plots were intriguing enough to keep me attached to the reading without all of the "junk" found in many mystery novels. Also, learning the customs, the religion, and the ways of the various Navajo tribes, within the Navajo nation, was intriguing. I guess I have all of Hillerman's novels. Hillerman, incidentally, is not Navajo. He is an Anglo who is a dedicated Catholic, but he thinks like a Navajo and understands the Navajo ways. And he is a piping good storyteller.

WHAT ABOUT YOU?

So, what will be your releasing activity or activities? *You don't have to be good at it. You do have to lose yourself in it.* It may be a hobby or something that used to be a hobby. You may just bump into it by accident, as Mary Jane Worden did with the releasing power of beauty. Anyone can do morning pages. It may be a good place to begin.

What are you trying to do through a releasing activity? You are trying to find an activity that will release your stressed-out mind and let it rest while you actively engage another part of your mind that is waiting to be used. Like many elements of the grief experience, this is not an event but a process. Seek and you will find!

****

This I Can Do Today:

I can begin to try to find something of such engaging interest and requiring such concentration that it will release my grief-bound mind.

This I Can Remember Today:

I can remember that there are parts of my mind that have not been damaged by what has happened.

CHAPTER SEVEN

Strength from beyond Yourself

A young doctor friend who was just out of medical school took his turn in the trauma unit of a large downtown hospital emergency room on Saturday nights. He treated injuries caused by accidents, gunshot wounds, and emergencies of all kinds. One Saturday night he asked me if I would like to come along. He put me through a sterilizing procedure—outfitted me with a mask, gown, and gloves—and allowed me to watch. For virtually everyone who was admitted, the nurses hung a container with some kind of fluid or plasma that flowed down the tubes and into the veins of the patient.

Once the young physician looked at me as the nurse was making all of this happen and said simply, "Instant life. Instant people!" Then with a twinkle in his eye, knowing I was a preacher, he said, "There is a parable here. If you've been in a life-threatening accident, you need help beyond yourself." He was absolutely right. It is a parable. It is a parable about accessing resources beyond yourself in the midst of deep grief.

To quote my doctor friend, "You need help beyond yourself." From where? As we have seen, our culture almost never assists us in the healing of our grief. Granger Westberg sums it up like this: "We conduct a quiet conspiracy of silence against it. We try never to talk about grief, and certainly never display it by any outward sign. We offer our sympathy to our grieving friends immediately after their loss has occurred, but from then on we say in effect, 'Now, let's get back to business as usual again.' "[1]

How do we, whose grief is so sharp and full of pain, find hope and healing?

I believe the wisdom of grief calls us to access strength from beyond ourselves. Spiritual strength is not earthbound or culturebound. It comes through the presence of God, who is able to walk with us through this dark night of the soul and give us the inner strength to make it. However, as physical strength in that emergency room came through plasma, tubes, and needles into the physical body, spiritual strength comes through three sources also: *Scripture, prayer, and insight.* The most rewarding way to do this is on a day-to-day basis. It could become for you a daily renewal time.

You may never have sought spiritual help before, or you may be an old hand at accessing spiritual resources. In any case, the following four prayers, scriptures, and insights are examples of how you can receive strength and power from beyond yourself. There are many more, of course. You can use again and again the ones that speak to you. I have also included exercises. They may seem awkward. But when you are alone, try them. They often help.

THE ACCEPTANCE PRAYER

The Serenity Prayer, or as I like to call it, the Acceptance Prayer, appears in mottos, on cards, and in many other places. It goes like this:

> God, give us grace to accept with serenity the things that cannot be changed, courage to change the things that should be changed, and the wisdom to distinguish the one from the other. Amen.[2]

One story behind the Serenity Prayer is that it had its origin in 1934 when a well-known theologian and preacher, Dr. Reinhold Niebuhr, wrote out the prayer on a small piece of paper and used it while leading Sunday worship at a church in the Northeast. After the service, a businessman asked to have a copy of it. Niebuhr is said to have reached into his pocket, handed it to the man, and said, "Here, you take it. I have no further use for it." The man put it on his Christmas cards that year. Others used it. The Red Cross picked it up during World War II. Its power has now reached across the world. Alcoholics Anonymous embraces it, as do many other groups.

I have changed the prayer to make it appropriate for one who has suffered great loss. Serenity is changed to acceptance. *Serenity* is not an appropriate word for grief. We are never serene. But acceptance is essential to our long-term hopefulness.

Lord, help me to accept the things I cannot change.

One of the major milestones in the grief journey is the acceptance of what has happened. Since the publication of the groundbreaking book by Elisabeth Kübler-Ross, almost everyone who has studied grief has pegged acceptance as a key factor in moving through the reality of loss to a sense of hopefulness.[3]

However, acceptance is not an event; it is a process. It is not a stage or a phase so much as it is little breakthroughs along the way, many of them spiritual. Beginning to accept what has happened is a journey upon which we embark, more than a destination we reach.

What does it mean to accept what can't be changed? It does *not* mean we forget what has happened and no longer carry the memories in our hearts. I think of a wonderful man who was pushing toward seventy years of age. He and his wife had moved to our city to be close to their son, who was a distinguished physician. Now they were facing a move to a retirement center and trying to get rid of some of what they had gathered through the years. Earlier in the week he had come home to find his wife weeping, sitting in a chair. He rushed to her to ask what was wrong. She could not speak, so she handed him a picture of their little daughter, whom they had lost more than forty years before. He said she was ten years old when she died. "Pastor," he said, "that has been decades ago. We no longer talk about it. Why is it still so fresh?" After some moments of quiet, he added, "On the other hand, I am so glad she is still part of our memory and our family." Accepting what can't be changed does not mean we forget, nor would we want to. What it does mean is that we have moved far enough into our grief to be able to get on with our lives.

Help me to change what needs to be changed.

But the Acceptance Prayer does not stop with acceptance. It speaks of changing some things: "Help me to change what needs to be changed." For instance, we can change a bitter attitude to one that is positive.

My friend Margaret knew trauma and sorrow like few do. She was one of those special "saints" who bore both with perseverance and grace. Those who had known her through the years had awarded her their deepest admiration.

One day a friend asked Margaret, "What is your secret? How have you carried so much for so long without it crushing you?" Margaret replied, "You are not the first to ask me that. I don't think I'm stronger than anyone else would have been under the circumstances. We all do what we have to do. But I have learned one thing through it all. I have learned that when we are grateful for the smallest of blessings, we are better able to carry the heaviest of loads."

That is a remarkable way of looking at things, an insightful change that can make a huge difference in our approach to the challenges of each day. Margaret's courageous insight was, "*I have learned that when we are grateful for the smallest of blessings, we are better able to carry the heaviest of loads."*

An Exercise

Sit down, close your eyes, and think about, even visualize, your life. Review blessings in your life for which you can be grateful but that you have overlooked. Think small and big. Remember Margaret's insight: when we are able to be grateful for the smallest of blessings, we are more able to carry the heaviest of loads. Now sincerely pray the substance of the Acceptance Prayer:

Lord, I really am trying to accept what can't be changed. Help me to change the way I look at things. May I begin to notice the smallest of blessings so I can better carry the heaviest of loads. Thank you. Amen.

SPIRITUAL HELP FOR AN UNCERTAIN FUTURE

The LORD himself goes before you and will be with you; he will never leave you nor forsake you. Do not be afraid; do not be discouraged. —Deuteronomy 31:8 (NIV)

These words are life-giving for me. I claimed them and believed them after our son died, and they got me through some of the toughest times. They come to us from Moses, the great leader behind the Hebrew exodus from slavery in Egypt. Their escape is told in the biblical book appropriately called Exodus. After more than forty years, the fledgling Hebrew nation finally arrived at the edge of the promised land.

On the eastward side of the Jordan River is a small mountain called Mount Nebo. It is not a high mountain as mountains go, but tall enough to look out into the promised land. It allowed Moses to look upon what he had dreamed of for so long. But this is not the younger, energetic leader who stood down the Egyptian pharaoh. Moses is at the end of his journey. God has told him to hand the leadership mantle over to Joshua, which he does. In what amounts to a farewell address he says good-bye to his people, a key part of which is Deuteronomy 31:8, quoted above. In summary Moses tells them never to forget that the Lord is with them and goes before them. Fear and discouragement will come. But they are not to let fear or discouragement take up residence in their hearts.

These words could just as well be addressed to you and me right now. Remember that the Lord, who is with you right now, goes before you and is walking ahead of you into the future. Receive his strength. Open your heart to his never-leaving presence. Especially hear the words: "Do not be afraid."

An Exercise

When you are by yourself, stand where you have room to pretend that you are in the middle of a circle. Now name the fears and anxieties that you carry around day by day, or even write them on slips of paper, and place them in a circle on the floor around you until you are surrounded by that circle of your fears and anxieties. Now use the words from Moses to form a prayer.

Lord, you have promised to go before me and to be with me. You have promised that you will never leave me or forsake me. I claim that promise right now. I truly believe you can help me to step beyond my fears and anxieties as I meet the responsibilities of today. Thank you, Lord. Amen.

Pause for a moment to absorb and believe that God can really help you. Now step over that circle of fears and anxieties, and leave them behind. Leave them behind! Leave them behind! Then turn strong to meet your day.

THE JESUS PRAYER

Join me as we imagine ourselves standing beside a man who was a blind beggar in the prosperous city of first-century Jericho. How would it feel to be a beggar, blind and helpless, in a city of wealth? The incident is recorded in the Bible in three Gospels, Matthew, Mark, and Luke, but Mark gives us this blind beggar's name. He is Bartimaeus, the son of Timaeus (Mark 10:46-52 RSV). It is possible that Mark knew his name because the two of them could have been part of a local fellowship of believers. What is incredible about his cry for help is that it has survived for twenty centuries as a prayer for mercy used by people like you and me.

After Jesus finished his teaching and was leaving Jericho, Bartimaeus was sitting by the roadside. He could not see, but his ears told him that Jesus was coming, followed by a large crowd. He had heard about Jesus, and he didn't hesitate to cry out, "Jesus, Son of David, have mercy on me!" The crowd around him tried to hush him up, but he cried out all the more. What did he have to lose?

He got the attention of Jesus, who called for him and asked, "What do you want me to do for you?" The reply was, "Master, let me receive my sight." The word for Master is the Hebrew word for Rabbi, which is what many of the people would have perceived Jesus to be. Jesus replied, "Go your way; your faith has made you well." Mark reports, "And immediately he received his sight and followed him" (Mark 10:52).

Later, when Christianity came to the Greco-Roman world, the prayer was changed for those who would not have known the significance of the Jewish title "Son of David." The Greco-Roman believers changed it to become like a confession of faith: "Jesus Christ, God's Son, Savior, have mercy on me." Then someone noticed that the first Greek letters of the first five words spelled out the Greek word for fish. The Greek word for fish in English sounds like *ickthus*. Thus the image of a fish became a secret symbol for believers.

For instance, suppose one man suspected that another man was a Christian. Because Roman persecution of Christians was ever present, "Are you a Christian?" was not a question to be asked or information to be shared. So the believer might kneel down and draw in the sand a half circle. If the other man was a believer, he would kneel down and complete the simple sketch of a fish by drawing a half circle the other way. Perhaps then the two would embrace because they knew they were Christian brothers in

Christ. Thus it was that the sign of the fish became a symbol of the Christian faith.

You see this symbol in interesting places today, for example, attached to the back of cars. Amazing. Two thousand years later the fish symbol survives, which says, "Jesus Christ, God's Son, Savior, have mercy on me."

I share with you my remarkable experience with this prayer. When our son was so ill and I walked the hospital halls, I found myself praying the Jesus Prayer like Bartimaeus prayed it: "Jesus, Son of David, have mercy on us." Using "Son of David" reminded me that Jesus was not only truly God but also fully human. As a human, he understood my need for mercy. The prayer became a huge comfort for me.

In later years I have come up with my own addition to the Jesus Prayer. It is the confession of faith of the early Christians but adds a line that includes the Lord as being our Shepherd, just like Psalm 23 does. With the shepherd addition, the Jesus Prayer goes like this:

Jesus Christ, God's Son, Savior, Shepherd of my life, have mercy on me.

This is an easy prayer to memorize. When your spirit is really down, you might pray it silently through the day. It is a cry for mercy like the one that Bartimaeus prayed so long ago. It reaches out for spiritual strength beyond yourself to the comfort and guidance of God.

An Exercise

Do some imaging. In your mind picture yourself alongside the blind beggar, Bartimaeus, who is crying out for help from beyond himself. Jesus calls for you as well as Bartimaeus to come to him. In your mind you kneel before him. Then he asks you the same question that he asked the blind beggar: "What do you want me to do for you?" Tell him. Unload on him if you need to. He has heard it all before. He really wants to be the Shepherd of your life. Close your prayer by being thankful for his presence and his mercy.

A SHORT PRAYER FOR A LONG DAY

After we lost our son, I felt I needed a prayer that wrapped its arms around my fears about the future but also addressed my daily responsibilities. It needed to be a short prayer, easily remembered, and one that I could pray silently throughout the day.

One day as I was reading the Psalms, I came across a phrase that seemed an answer to my fears about the horizons ahead. The line is from King David, who wrote these words during especially difficult times: "My times are in your hands" (Ps. 31:15 NIV). By the way, Jesus quoted from this Psalm from the cross: "Into your hands I commit my spirit" (Psalm 31:5; Luke 23:46 NIV).

When we open ourselves to God and pray, "My times are in your hands," we are releasing our past, present, and future to his keeping. There are times when we pray this prayer of commitment that we can feel the anxiety lift and began to shift our attention to what is going on today.

That brings us to the second line of this short prayer. It has to do with the present. It embraces not only today, not only this hour, but this very moment! I encountered this concept of focusing on the duties of every moment when I was reading the book *Devotional Classics* by Richard J. Foster and James Bryan Smith.[4] The concept came from a man I had never heard of until then, Jean-Pierre de Caussade. He lived in France in the eighteenth century. One of the things he wrote about was a new concept of time that he called "the sacrament of the present moment." A sacrament for Christians is something that serves as a means of God's grace. The most well-known sacraments are baptism and the celebration of the Last Supper (also called Communion or the Eucharist). Jean-Pierre widened the concept of sacrament to include not just time in general but making the duty of every moment a sacrament. De Caussade would insist that cooking a meal, washing dishes, fulfilling responsibilities at work, or helping the children with their homework were all duties that could become like sacraments for us. When we give to God the duty of every moment, God answers with the strength to carry out our duties. The sacrament of every moment will make a change in the way you look at your duties.

Now let's try to bring together these two lines, one from King David and one from Jean-Pierre de Caussade. Incidentally, David lived 1000 B.C. while Jean-Pierre de Caussade lived A.D. 1700. That makes them 2,700 years apart, but together in a prayer. Indeed it is true: our times are in God's hands!

O Lord,

My times are in your hands.

Help me give myself to the duties of the present moment.

In the name and strength of Jesus. Amen.

Often when I have prayed this prayer, I have found release from my worries and fears about the future. But I have also found strength beyond myself to focus on the tasks and duties of every day. Such moments have truly become sacraments for me.

An Exercise

Open your hands and pretend you are putting your future in one palm and the present moment in the other. Now close your hands tightly. You hold in your grip the future and the present moments of your life. You are, as it were, keeping them tightly to yourself. At this point they are totally yours.

Now, in an act of trusting commitment, release them and let them go by opening your hands and handing them to God. You are handing your past and future to God with one opened hand. You are handing the duties of the present moment to God with the other hand even as he blesses you with new strength.

****

This I Can Do Today:

I can pray throughout the day a short prayer I have memorized.

This I Can Remember Today:

I can remember that being grateful for the smallest blessings can help me carry the heaviest loads.

CHAPTER EIGHT

Living with Your
Questions

In the best of times an exclamation mark is often the best
punctuation we can give to a faith that is secure and bristles
with hope. We can do it! Have faith! All things are possible
with God! Keep up your hope! Keep praying because God answers
prayers! Believe! Trust! Ask!

BUT WHAT HAPPENS WHEN THINGS
FALL APART?

When Dave's leukemia went into remission, we were grateful
but not surprised. Our deep conviction was that our prayers had
been answered. But five months later when he came out of remission, we were wiped out. It was December 1, a date I will never forget. I was looking out the window when Dave and his wife, Betsy,

drove up, having returned from the checkup. As they got out of the car, I knew from their posture what the report had been. The doctor later told us that having come out of remission, Dave had a minimal chance of a cure. He also told us that Dave had the toughest kind of leukemia. We lost him three months later.

We were devastated. We had believed! We had trusted! We had hoped! We had prayed! One regret I have is that I never said good-bye to Dave. I never thought I would have to. Then he went into a coma, and I didn't have a chance. We did pray and people all over the world prayed. We had claimed the promises we had taken from Scripture. But healing never happened. Why?

In the coming days, weeks, and months our exclamation marks were replaced with question marks. The punctuation of our spirits had changed.

- Why had our prayers not been answered?
- Why Dave? Why us?
- What about the promises we had learned from the Bible about answered prayer and God's looking out for us?

When the full impact of grief hit us, we become acutely aware of how fragile we really were. How quickly things changed when the chilly winds of loss came our way.

When tragedy comes we will live with questions. Why? Why didn't God answer our prayers? What could we have done differently? Where is God in all of this? If we ever make peace with the loss that we face, we will have to embrace some answer to *why*. In the meantime we learn to live with the questions. I remember Rose Kennedy's answer when two of her sons, John and Robert, were assassinated. John was President and Robert was a senator. Her answer was, "It was the will of God." That was the way she made peace with her tragedy. Your answer may not be hers, but you will find yourself groping for an answer to "why?" Where is God in all of this? Sometimes the answer is not so much intellectual as it is spiritual. My wife Shirley's answer to our loss was that she came to a place where she could forgive God.

Philip Yancey's Answer

The well-known author Philip Yancey heard disappointment often in the notes and letters he received about an earlier book he had written, *Where Is God When It Hurts?*[1] He decided to write a book about it, *Disappointment with God.*[2] His is one of the best discussions of the Old Testament book of Job that I know of anywhere. His understanding of the biblical picture of God is superb.

In the book he tells of holing up in a Colorado cabin to ponder what had been shared with him through the months and years. He brought many books but wound up reading only the Bible. He read it straight through, cover to cover. When he started, the Colorado snow had started to fall. When he reached Deuteronomy, snow covered the bottom step. When he got to the Prophets, it had crept up the mailbox post. When he finished the last chapter of Revelation, he had to call for a snowplow!

What Yancey came to realize, and what many of us wounded by life have come to affirm, is that the God we were taught about in religion class has little similarity with the God in the Bible. Yancey writes,

> I had learned to think of God as an unchanging, invisible spirit who possesses such qualities as omnipotence, omniscience, and impassibility (incapable of emotion). . . . Simply reading the Bible, I encountered not a misty vapor but an actual Person. A Person as unique and distinctive and colorful as any person I know. God has deep emotions; he feels delight and frustration and anger.

The doctrinal image of God and the personal image of God are not alike. Yancey states, "By studying 'about' God, by taming him and reducing him to words . . . I had lost the force of the passionate relationship God seeks above all else . . . a God who wants desperately to love and be loved by us."[3]

People without Faith Suffer Also

If faith needs to be healed, is faith a liability in the time of loss? I would absolutely disagree. People who have little or no faith wind up dealing with the same realities that believers do, and they have minimal or no spiritual resources to help them move through the loss and despair.

Years ago, one observing Victor Hugo, when informed of his daughter's death, described it this way:

> A moment back I had seen him smiling and happy, and now, in the space of a second, without the slightest transition, he seemed as though thunderstruck. His poor lips were white; his magnificent eyes were staring in front of him. His face and his hair were wet with tears. His poor hand was pressed to his heart as though to keep it from bursting from his breast.[4]

For others, all that they have to build on is their doubts.

In the poem "After the Burial," written after one of his daughters died, James Russell Lowell wrote:

In the breaking gulfs of sorrow,
When the helpless feet stretch out
And find in the deeps of darkness
No footing so solid as doubt.[5]

It is one thing to face the need to heal faith and another to have no faith to heal.

So how is your wounded faith healed? Usually it begins with the acceptance that it is not God you are rejecting but your *image* of God. You will have to work with and through your image of God. You may need to rethink it until you have peace. The important thing is to face it and walk through it, not around it. Søren Kierkegaard, a devoted Christian, said that Christians often reminded him of schoolboys who want to look up the answers to their math problems in the back of the book rather than work them through.

In working with my disappointment I realized I needed healing on two fronts. I needed first to deal with my grieving heart. But eventually I needed to address my disappointed mind. The following is a brief summary of my understanding of *why*. But you will have to walk your own journey here.

Human Choice and the Advent of Evil

God is the key reality in my life. But I tended to overlook two huge influences that crowd around human events as well. There are others, of course, but these are the two that often impact tragic happenings.

Review with me that wonderfully profound story at the very beginning of the Bible (Gen. 1–3). Adam and Eve are set up in a magnificent garden. No problems. No challenges. *Then God changes everything. God wills that Adam and Eve shall have a will.* He chooses to give them the power to choose. You might say, "Okay. We can choose. What's the big deal?" Focus with me on what we are dealing with. Neither you nor I can impose what we will, what we choose, upon another person unless he or she is willing. We cannot make another person love us unless he or she is willing. When God willed that we should have a will, he limited his control and, in that sense, outcomes.

Then for Adam and Eve, God sets up a choice tree, which is an invisible but automatic feature of any boundary. He says, "Eat any fruit anywhere in the garden but not of this tree, which is the knowledge of good and evil."

God tells them what he wants, what they should want, and leaves. He leaves them free to choose! Human freedom is born. Apparently God prefers freedom above absolute control. With freedom God sets the stage for the world to become a very messy affair indeed. Here is a good question that will give your mind pause: Did God make a mistake by giving us freedom? Of course, if freedom goes, so does love.

Evil Enters

In the biblical story, evil enters with human freedom. Into that magnificent garden of innocence the Satan-serpent appears and calls into question everything God said. His main thrust is that God was so insecure he was afraid that they, Adam and Eve, would become like he was. Satan promises that if they go ahead and eat the fruit, they will become superior beings; they will become like God. Adam and Eve buy into the pitch of the Satan-serpent. They eat the fruit that they hope will make them superior beings, which is the basic temptation that Satan always brings. It reminds me of a young man who refuses to give up smoking marijuana because it makes him feel superior. He also insists that the reason "older people" are against it is that they are afraid younger people will become superior. Sound familiar? For Adam and Eve, consequences happen immediately. They lose their innocence, clothe themselves, hide from God, and are forced to leave the garden.

Wow! What changes have been made in the garden of innocence. The freedom to choose and the power of evil to influence infiltrate that beautiful garden with huge consequences. There is an apt saying: "We have met the enemy and he is us!" But if we dare to examine the Genesis story, the enemy is not only us but also evil. Incidentally, ours is an age that loves choices but hates consequences. In the Genesis account and in our contemporary life, they go together.

In my pilgrimage of trying to figure out why bad things happen to good people, the Genesis story of the beginnings of human choice and the reality of evil play a significant role. But before you or I despair, there is a wonderful plus when it comes to human choice.

The Positive Side of Choice: Love

Choice opens the door to evil. It also opens the door to love. The lifeblood of love is choice. God, who is love, would rather risk wrong choices than forfeit the possibility that we might choose to love him *in spite of* rather than *only because of.*

We read in 1 John 4:8 that "God is love." God wants us to love him and wants to love us, but love requires at least two, two who have chosen to love each other. No amount of willpower can make another person love us if he or she doesn't want to. God knows that, and he runs the huge risk of rejection with Adam, Eve, and the rest of us. But how much pleasure and joy it must give God when we love not only because of but in spite of.

Douglas John Hall sums it up so well: "God's problem is not that God *is not able* to do certain things. God's problem is that God loves. Love complicates the life of God as it complicates every life."[6]

THE HEALING TOUCHES OF GOD'S POWER

In the healing of my faith I found myself asking, *What are the healing touches of God that heal our faith and make it strong again?*

God's Presence

For me, the first touch was God's presence. Many have written of God's absence in the midst of grief. I understand that. I have had periods in my life when God seemed nowhere—near or far. But as I walked sorrow's path, I always had the sense that the presence of God was there. My frustration was that the healing wasn't happening. Yet the presence was always there.

The healing of faith requires us to accept that *we are not going to understand everything and that God is present whether or not we feel the presence.* The presence of God tends to reside in our hearts, while our intellectual understanding resides in our heads. Both are important. But as Paul says in 1 Corinthians 13, we know in part. He says it twice in case we miss it. And in case we need an image, he provides that. We see as in a mirror, dimly, or to use the older translation, through a glass darkly. We will never fully understand the problem of evil and suffering because we know in part. Some part or perception is always missing. I will never understand why Dave wasn't healed. I can accept it as something I cannot understand and cannot change. I do believe that cancer is evil and outside the will of God.

But here is a wonderful balance to our partial understanding of God. We don't have to understand all about God to be healed by his presence. We do experience God's presence in part, but that part is more than enough. Now, all of these years later, I realize his presence was nothing more than the fulfillment of the Lord's promise: "And surely I am with you always, to the very end of the age" (Matt. 28:20 NIV).

God's Love

The second touch was the overwhelming sense of God's love. I might not understand why healing did not take place, but I was aware of God's presence and love through it all. Even now I pause in reverence and gratitude that the love of God was present to sustain me and all of the family during that period.

You might ask, "If God loved you, why did he let Dave die?" My answer would be that ultimately, we have a choice between believing in a controlling, in-charge-of-everything God or a God of love. Love can control but often does not. Love does set boundaries. But love also allows the boundaries to be transgressed. Love allows. Love forgives. Love also grieves. Sensitive parents live with the same realities that God does.

As a result of his Colorado retreat, Philip Yancey wrote, "I had a strong sense that God doesn't care so much about being analyzed. Mainly he wants to be loved. Nearly every page of his Word rustles with this message. And I returned home knowing I must somehow explore the relationship between a passionate God—hungry for the love of his people—and the people themselves."[7]

Surprised by a Crucifix

The healing of faith, like the healing of relationships, often happens in sudden and unpredictable ways.

One day I chanced to be at home alone. At that time we had Dave and Betsy's children with us, and healing moments of great joy happened when we were with them. On that day I don't remember where everyone else was nor do I remember what I was doing. I do remember how much I was hurting inside. I was walking through the living room when I passed by an antique crucifix that my wife had purchased. Shirley knew I didn't believe a crucifix was the best way to approach faith, but she explained that it was a beautiful piece of art. I accepted her judgment. She had placed it on the mantel.

I must have passed by that crucifix hundreds of times. But on that day the portrayal of Christ on the cross caught the corner of my eye and captured me. I sat down. I was overcome with the portrayal of Christ on the cross. Tears came. The more I looked, the more I cried. I believe the Spirit knew where I was and what I needed. I needed to be reminded that the Christ that I served was "a man of sorrows, and acquainted with grief," as Isaiah described him (Isa. 53:3 KJV). Suddenly I knew deep down that the Lord knew where I was. He had been there. His suffering was a million times more than mine. But the important thing in that moment was that I knew that God, as I know him in Jesus, knew where I was and what I was going through. I was embraced by both the love and the presence of God.

Later I could smile at myself and at the humor of the Spirit. As I said, I didn't even believe in portraying Christ on a crucifix. I wonder how many times I have said, "Why do they leave him on the cross? He isn't there. He is risen!" I rejoiced when Catholic hospitals replaced the traditional crucifix with what they call the ascension cross, portraying Christ with his hands raised toward heaven, not nailed to the cross.

But on that day I needed the priceless gift of a suffering Savior whose wounds could begin to heal me from his cross. Now, nailed to my cross of loss, I was sitting there sobbing. I looked at that crucifix as it portrayed Jesus' nailed hands and feet and his head drooping in pain. What I knew then and what I know now is that my Lord knew where I was and that he was weeping with me.

How often God heals our faith in this way. He comes in the back door of our consciousness. When we least expect it, in unsuspecting ways, the Spirit opens our hearts to the love of the Father and the suffering of the Son. How often it comes at unlikely times and in unlikely places. How often the Holy Spirit uses what we, knowing in part and believing in part, had previously rejected.

Such experiences are stepping-stones to the rebuilding of our faith. God is the God of great surprises, and he sometimes brings a surprise gift even in our grief. Here is something you may never have thought of: the God who created the possibility of faith in the first place by giving Adam and Eve the power to choose is even more interested in rebuilding your faith than you are. Stay open to possibilities.

The Healing of Faith

We all have heard of faith healers. In this chapter we have dealt with the healing of our faith. Most of the healing of grief has to do with our emotions and our memories of the past. But we also have to face our questions. Why? Why us? What about the promises of God? There are no easy answers, nor is there any one answer. "We know in part," says the Apostle Paul. But the wisdom of grief comes to us eventually to say, "It is time to make peace with your questions. Don't walk around them. Walk through them. The wounds in your mind need attention. To fully walk into the future, you need to face the questions of the past."

****

This I Can Do Today:

I can begin to make peace with my questions, knowing that God will be with me as I struggle through them.

This I Can Remember Today:

The Lord identifies with me in my loss. He is "a man of sorrows, and acquainted with grief."

CHAPTER NINE

Turning Points and Beginning Again

The experience of grief takes us down many paths. In time, the emotions of painful grief move into a gentler expression, a quiet sadness. The sadness is, in its own way, a tribute. It says about the one who is gone, "You were such an essential part of my life that I will never forget you." However, the quiet sadness is often a signal that, without betraying the past, you have come to a turning point. The wisdom of grief may be saying, "The worst is over. A measure of healing has happened. Take a quiet look inward. Look forward as well as backward." These might be called *turning points*.

TURNING POINTS

Turning points often happen when we least expect them. Our job situation may suddenly change, family matters have intervened, or a health crisis comes our way. Given a change in our situation, we have no choice but to look at the future instead of the past.

However, turning points also happen when our situation has remained steady but *we ourselves* have changed. Grief has done enough of its healing to allow some changes within us. A friend shared with me this experience. After his son died, his outlook was that everything had turned gray—not literal gray, but colorless. He went on with his life, his schedule, his business. Months passed and then a year and another year. Then one day he noticed color. He smiled. He was seeing color again. In my walk with grief it was well into the third year that I was driving down a tree-laden street I often travel. I noticed I was whistling. It was a nice shock, a nice surprise. I hadn't whistled in forever. I had reached a turning point. The wisdom of grief was saying to me, "Healing has happened. It is time to be grateful for the past but start looking ahead to the future."

The Turning Points of Naomi and Ruth

An excellent example of life's turning points is the brief story of Ruth from the Old Testament. It is told in only four chapters in the book that bears her name and carries a huge amount of grief within its story line. Yet God works in and through virtually everything that happens. Ruth and Naomi truly reach turning points and begin again.

The story begins with a crisis in the land of Judah in and around Bethlehem where both King David and Jesus were born, although a thousand years apart. Famine has come. There is no food. There is no rain in sight. A man by the name of Elimelech asks himself, *What am I going to do? My family will starve unless I do something.* His family includes his wife, Naomi, and their two sons, Mahlon and Chilion. It is also possible that their two sons were not strong, husky young men. Mahlon means "sickly," and Chilion means "frail."[1] Elimelech makes a momentous decision. He decides to move to Moab, a country east of the Dead Sea. Moabites didn't like Jews and Jews didn't like Moabites. But the land of Moab had food. Elimelech and his family move to Moab. They settle in. Things go well. The two sons fall in love and marry two Moabite women: Ruth and Orpah. Elimelech, it appears, has made a wise move. His family has survived. His sons have married. They have lived there ten years when things come unraveled.

First, Elimelech dies, which is bad enough. But both of his two sons die also. Naomi, Ruth, and Orpah are widows! Ruth and Orpah can survive. They are Moabites and young. Naomi? She is a Jewess and growing older. Naomi is at a turning point and wonders, *What am I going to do now that I am a widow in a foreign land?* The word comes that the famine has been broken in Judah. She decides to return to the country of her birth.

Ruth and Orpah are also at turning points. They must now ask, "What are we going to do?" All three of them start toward Judah, but Naomi appeals to them to go back and put their roots down in Moab. Orpah follows Naomi's advice and turns toward home. In contrast, Ruth commits herself to Naomi in some of the most beautiful Hebrew in the Old Testament:

> Don't urge me to leave you or to turn back from you. Where you go I will go, and where you stay I will stay. Your people will be my people and your God my God. Where you die I will die,

and there I will be buried. May the LORD deal with me, be it ever so severely, if anything but death separates you and me. (Ruth 1:16-17 NIV)

When Naomi and Ruth arrive in Bethlehem, they create quite a stir.

"Can this be Naomi?" the women in the community ask. But Naomi won't let them call her by her birth name because the meaning of Naomi is "pleasant." She insists they call her Mara, which means "bitter."[2] Loss has taken its toll.

All the story thus far is squeezed into the first chapter of a four-chapter book! The other three chapters are a wonderful love story between Ruth and Boaz, who is a kinsman of Naomi. Ruth and Boaz fall in love and marry. Ruth bears a son who becomes the absolute delight of Grandmother Naomi. They name him Obed, who becomes the father of Jesse, who is the father of David (Ruth 4:21-22). Ruth, a Moabite, becomes King David's great-grandmother! That is not all. Through David, Ruth becomes part of the lineage, the family tree, of Jesus. Matthew traces this lineage in the first chapter of his Gospel (Matt. 1:5-6, 16).

Who would have thought that anything good could have been squeezed out of the story of grief and tragedy that embraced Naomi and Ruth? Who could ever have imagined that Ruth, a foreigner from the hated Moab, could provide part of the heritage of King David and Jesus?

Options during Turning Points

Both Naomi and Ruth handle their turning points well. They act. They are not frozen or immobilized because of the challenges they face. Such moments call forth crucial decisions for all of us when we get there. We can stay frozen where we are, in which case we can begin to shrivel up as persons. The loss we have experienced continues to be the major horizon of our lives. We forget that grief has healed us for a purpose. Not that we will forget the person for whom we grieve. That is not an option. The memories and the sadness will be with us the rest of our lives to some extent. The question is, Do we want that to be the horizon of our lives forever?

We need to remind ourselves that the one for whom we grieve would want us to get on with our lives. He or she would want us to pick up life when we are able and get on with what we are put on earth to do.

What Is at Stake?

How do we turn from a survival mode to a move-ahead mode? How do we turn from a focus on healing the wounds of the past to looking ahead to the possibilities of the present and future? A good place to begin is to recognize what is at stake in decisions we make at a turning point in our lives.

Dick Leider knew John Williamson as a friend and colleague. John was a graduate of Harvard, a leader, a teacher, and a leading thinker on change and cutting-edge technology. Cancer invaded his future. On the last day before the cancer claimed victory, Dick was privileged to spend some time with him. They laughed and wept together, talking of times past and of their work together. Dick thought of the time that John, with a pack on his back, so alive and alert to every opportunity, had interacted with the Masai in Africa. What a contrast to the immobility of the present.

As John stared out the window, struggling to see with his one remaining good eye, he said to Dick, "I always thought God had a plan for me to do something special in this life, but I never really found out what it was. I feel as if I never really found out who I wanted to be when I grew up." The tears came from both of them. His closing words were meant to encourage Dick in his work. "Push them to make a difference," he said, "and don't let them off the hook." John died the next day.[3]

"*Push them to make a difference and don't let them off the hook.*"

I wonder if we who have suffered heartbreaking grief are "off the hook" when it comes to making a difference? Dick also shares a frightening comment about other people he has known and talked with. He relates that many people walk through life feeling desperate: "They are grieving over the loss of a life—their own."[4] Even though we have suffered great loss, we do not want to close out our lives feeling we haven't really lived them. That would be a double loss. Not only will we have lost the one we loved, but we can lose our own lives by closing them down.

We who walk the grief path must live with two equally strong truths:

1. The first is that we must honor our grief. Grief is an invisible healer that prepares us to get on with our lives. Furthermore, the wisdom of grief tells us that healing

cannot be rushed. The wisdom of grief teaches us to treasure what has been, to turn loss into a tribute.

2. We must honor a second truth. At an appropriate pivot point in our grief, we begin to feel that we must get on with our lives. We have been focused on what happened in the past, focused on healing the deep loss we have experienced. But at a certain turning point we must realize we need two sets of glasses, one that looks at the past in tribute and in gratitude, and the other that looks at our present needs and our future possibilities. We do not want to be grieving over the loss of another life—our own.

BEGINNING AGAIN

Suppose we were at a restaurant enjoying a meal and in the course of our conversation you asked me, "How can I discover what I am called to do with the rest of my life? How do I learn to walk confidently into the future?" I might reply, "If I write some things down on paper, will you promise to at least try them?" You nod yes. So I pull out a scratch pad or even use a paper napkin and write out seven things to consider as you look toward the future. These seven will help you focus on your purpose here on earth. They are seven steps often involved in beginning again.

1. Unpack Your Life's Unnecessary Stuff

One phrase often used in seminars these days is taken from the practices of participants who frequently pack and unpack as they travel. It is a graphic picture when it is applied to our lives.

We need to unpack the unnecessary stuff we carry around in our minds and hearts: hurts, hates, fears, failures, and frustrations. We need to unpack memories of choices we have made that we shouldn't have, and choices we didn't make that we should have, and so on and so on. In the language of faith we often speak of "emptying yourself before God so you can create space to be filled with spiritual direction and joy."

To some degree, this has already happened to us. When we walk through heavy grief, a by-product is that we tend to get rid of a lot of inner stuff we have been carrying around needlessly. *Grief has a way of thinning things out.* Things that were crucially important for us in earlier days don't matter at all now. Dreams dreamed in an earlier year may be irrelevant. Goals set "back when" may now seem trivial. Grief empties us as the process of healing happens. But some negative baggage is still within us. If we have to unpack some of this stuff again and again, let's do it.

Here is a tough truth: *Until you make peace with what has been, you risk ruining what can be.* With the help of a counselor, you can unpack that which festers deep within. Or you may rise early to write, to put it all down on paper. The more days you do this, the more unnecessary baggage will be emptied. It will help if you take what you have written and turn it over to the grace and forgiveness of God.

2. Make a True Commitment to New Beginnings

In the passage mentioned earlier, Ruth commits herself to newness all of the way around. She has been through a huge amount of grief. Her father-in-law dies, and then her own husband passes away. Whatever she does is going to be a new beginning. She decides to stick with Naomi, and in that commitment she packs her life full of new beginnings: "Where you go, I will go. Where you lodge, I will lodge. Your people will become my people. Your God will become my God."

God seems to have an affinity for new beginnings. At the beginning of the Bible, God is creating that which is new (Gen. 1–2). At the end of the Bible, God is pledging to create a new heaven and a new earth and make all things new (Rev. 21:1-5).

3. Identify Your Core Relationships

In the Ruth story, Ruth is nowhere without Naomi. Naomi becomes the bridge to other relationships, including that with Boaz. In your mind identify the four or five friends to whom you can go with joys, sorrows, and decisions. You consider them to be wise and supportive. They also have the ability to listen and keep confidences. A secular manual calls them your Personal Board of Directors.[5] You can trust these people. Probably they will never meet together as a group. They may not even know each other. But they know you well and you know them well, and that is what matters.

When you face a major decision, you can call them and set up a time to have lunch and talk. When you call to set it up, extend the courtesy to let them know what it is about: "I'm facing a major decision, and I need your counsel if you can spare the time." Or you may not be making a decision at all but just need time with a friend. I think of that German saying I used in an earlier chapter: "Don't go too far all alone." Identify your core relationships, and keep in touch with them without becoming a nuisance.

4. Keep an Inner Renewal Time Daily

Pay attention to the needs of your inner life. If you don't, nobody will. It is crucial. The everyday duties and demands of life can become so overwhelming that your inner self becomes impoverished. Find the things that nourish you and replenish you, the sources of your inner strength. Unpack your inmost needs and desires before God and then learn how to listen. In the previous chapter we talked about how you can do this.

5. Unpack Your Talents

You may not have thought about your talents for a long time. It is time to look within the baggage of your life and rediscover the gifts, the callings, the talents that are yours.

One mistake that we tend to make in identifying our talents is thinking of them as something we do. Rightly so. Action is required. But talents have more to do with who we are than with what we do. As you begin to search for your personal talents, here are some things that might help in the process:

1. What do you do superbly but easily?
2. If you were to ask your friends about your talents, perhaps your relational core people, what would they say, almost without thinking? Well, ask them.
3. What replenishes you? A true talent may take energy from you, but it also puts it back and you feel renewed.
4. What are you enthusiastic about? The English word *enthusiasm* comes from the Greek word *entheos*, which

is literally "in God." God's purpose for your life often surfaces in what you get excited about.

There are times when you may be offered positions in differing vocations. You may want to take another look at your talents before you decide.

6. Pay Attention to Attitudes

Grief and sadness go together. They should. Loss is real and final. But turning points are appropriate times to feel the pulse of your attitudes. This does not mean you have to smile continuously, but smiles are barometers of where you are and how you feel. I read an article noting that the average worker smiles twelve times a day. How would the article writer know? How could the writer count or gauge it? But just suppose that information is correct. That would mean there is not much joy circulating. In addition, having a commitment to others energizes our attitudes. Happy people are seldom self-centered people.

7. Write Your Future Fifteen

A final suggestion for a turning point in your life is to ask yourself, *What are fifteen things I would like to accomplish before I die?* I don't remember where this suggestion came from, but I filed it in my memory. It surfaced a decade ago when I was in the hospital for cancer surgery. Sitting in bed wondering whether the surgeon got it all seemed a pretty dour way to spend the day. So I got some paper and went to work on my Future Fifteen. Throughout the day, I added or scratched out items. When I finished, I slipped it into my Bible, where I thought it would not get lost.

I have looked at that Future Fifteen during these last years. It is an amazing list. I have accomplished about half of it. When a person has been carrying around a cancer, something is needed to pull him into the future and its dreams. If fifteen are not enough or too many, do your own thing. Keep your list around, and review it every now and then. Remember where you were when you wrote them down. Give God thanks for what has been accomplished. Take a deep breath and then walk into the future to accomplish what you haven't even started.

BEGIN AGAIN

Just as Ruth and Naomi discovered, you will reach a turning point and it will be time to begin again. It is a time not to forget the past but to realize that healing has taken place to get you where you are. It is a time not to forget the one you have lost but to realize that person would want you to get on with your life. What are your Future Fifteen?

****

This I Can Do Today:

I can consider whether I am at a turning point and a time to begin again.

This I Can Remember Today:

I can remember that God works in all things, past, present, and future, just as God did with Ruth and Naomi.

Notes

1. When Grief Breaks In

1. Nicholas Wolterstorff, *Lament for a Son* (Grand Rapids: Eerdmans, 1987), 15.

2. Granger E. Westberg, *Good Grief* (Philadelphia: Fortress, 1971), 46.

2. What Do I Do Now?

1. Harold S. Kushner, *When Bad Things Happen to Good People* (New York: Avon Books, 1981).

2. Ann Kaiser Stearns, *Coming Back* (New York: Ballantine, 1988), 20.

3. Unpredictable Emotions of Grief

1. Kenneth R. Mitchell and Herbert Ernest Anderson, *All Our Losses, All Our Griefs* (Louisville: Westminster John Knox Press, 1983), 64.

2. John Bramblett, *When Good-bye Is Forever: Learning to Live Again after the Loss of a Child* (New York: Ballantine, 1991), 21.

3. Ibid., 78.

4. John Bowlby, *Loss*, 2d. ed. (New York: Basic Books, HarperCollins, 1980).

5. C. S. Lewis, *A Grief Observed* (San Francisco: Harper, 1961), 15.

6. Tom Crider, *A Broken Heart Still Beats*, ed. Anne McCracken and Mary Semel (Center City, Minn.: Hazelden, 1998), 59.

7. Daniel G. Bagby, *Seeing through Our Tears* (Minneapolis: Augsburg Fortress, 1999), 54.

8. Ibid., 7.

4. Decide Whom to Talk To

1. Kenneth R. Mitchell and Herbert Ernest Anderson, *All Our Losses, All Our Griefs* (Louisville: Westminster John Knox Press, 1983), 98.

2. C. S. Lewis, *A Grief Observed* (San Francisco: Harper, 1961), 13–14.

3. Carol S. Pearson, *The Hero Within* (San Francisco: Harper & Row, 1989), 103.

4. Ann Kaiser Stearns, *Coming Back* (New York: Ballantine, 1989), 118.

5. When One Day at a Time Is Too Much

1. Gerald Mann, *When One Day at a Time Is Too Long* (New York: McCracken Press, 1994), 5.

2. Quoted by Kenneth R. Mitchell and Herbert Ernest Anderson, *All Our Losses, All Our Griefs* (Louisville: Westminster John Knox Press, 1983), 71.

6. Find Your Releasing Activities

1. Winston Churchill, *Painting as a Pastime* (New York: Cornerstone Library, 1965), 7–8.

2. Julia Cameron, *The Artist's Way* (New York: Penguin-Putnam, 1992), 9–18.

3. Julia Cameron, *The Vein of Gold* (New York: Penguin-Putnam, 1996), 13–17.

4. From Madeleine L'Engle's foreword to C. S. Lewis's *A Grief Observed* (San Francisco: Harper, 1961), 8.

5. Mary Jane Worden, from the *Women's Devotional Bible* (Grand Rapids: Zondervan, 1990), 1381.

6. Ibid.

7. Strength from beyond Yourself

1. Granger Westberg, *Good Grief* (Philadelphia: Fortress, 1972), 42.

2. Robert McAfee Brown, *The Essential Reinhold Niebuhr* (New Haven: Yale University Press, 1987), 251.

3. Elisabeth Kübler-Ross, *On Death and Dying* (New York: Macmillan, 1969), 112–37. She studied the responses of persons who were terminally ill and saw them going through five phases. Acceptance was the fifth and final stage.

4. Richard J. Foster and James Bryan Smith, *Devotional Classics* (San Francisco: HarperSanFrancisco, 1993), 230–35.

8. Living with Your Questions

1. Philip Yancey, *Where Is God When It Hurts?* (Grand Rapids: Zondervan, 1977).

2. Philip Yancey, *Disappointment with God* (New York: HarperCollins, 1988).

3. Ibid., 48.

4. Quoted from *A Broken Heart Still Beats*, ed. Anne McCracken and Mary Semel (Center City, Minn.: Hazelden, 1998), 15.

5. Ibid., 213.

6. Douglas John Hall, *God and Human Suffering* (Minneapolis: Augsburg, 1986), 156.

7. Yancey, *Disappointment with God*, 50.

9. Turning Points and Beginning Again

1. *The New Oxford Annotated Bible*, ed. Michael D. Coogan (New York: Oxford University Press, 2001), 392.

2. Ibid., 393.

3. Richard J. Leider and David A. Shapiro, *Repacking Your Bags* (San Francisco: Berrett-Koehler, 1996), 89–90.

4. Ibid., 6.

5. Ibid., 153